Mindful Emotional Intelligence

Achieving Balance through Mindfulness Practices and Embracing Self-Awareness and Compassion for a Fulfilling Life

Elise Little

Table of Contents

Introduction

In a world that moves at an increasingly fast pace, the ability to remain centered, compassionate, and self-aware has never been more crucial. Our daily lives are often filled with stress, distractions, and emotional turbulence that can leave us feeling disconnected from ourselves and others. In such a landscape, the practice of mindfulness offers a powerful tool to reclaim our sense of balance and inner peace. When combined with emotional intelligence, mindfulness becomes even more potent, enabling us to navigate the complexities of our emotions with clarity and empathy.

Mindful Emotional Intelligence is not just a concept; it's a way of living that can transform the way you relate to yourself and the world around you. By merging the ancient wisdom of mindfulness with the modern understanding of emotional intelligence, we can develop a deeper awareness of our emotions, thoughts, and behaviors. This awareness allows us to respond to life's challenges with greater insight and kindness, rather than reacting out of habit or impulse.

This book is a journey into the heart of mindful emotional intelligence. Whether you are new to mindfulness or have practiced for years, you will find practical guidance and actionable strategies to enhance your emotional intelligence through mindfulness practices. Each chapter is designed to help you cultivate self-awareness, manage your emotions with compassion, and build healthier, more fulfilling relationships.

You will learn how to:

- Develop a deeper understanding of your emotions and how they influence your thoughts and actions.

- Practice mindfulness techniques that ground you in the present moment, reducing stress and increasing emotional resilience.
- Cultivate compassion for yourself and others, fostering stronger connections and more meaningful interactions.
- Use mindful emotional intelligence to navigate difficult situations with grace and wisdom.

By the end of this book, you will have the tools to achieve a balanced and fulfilling life, one that is rooted in self-awareness, compassion, and mindful living. The journey you are about to embark on is not just about acquiring knowledge; it's about transforming your life from the inside out. Together, we will explore the path to mindful emotional intelligence, and in doing so, discover the profound peace and fulfillment that comes from living with greater awareness and intention.

Welcome to a new chapter of your life—one where mindfulness and emotional intelligence come together to create harmony within and around you.

Chapter 1: Understanding Emotional Intelligence

The Concept of Emotional Intelligence

Emotional intelligence (EI) is a term that has gained significant attention in recent years, yet its roots stretch back to the ancient understanding of human emotions and behaviors. At its core, emotional intelligence refers to the ability to recognize, understand, and manage our own emotions, as well as the emotions of others. Unlike traditional intelligence, which is measured by cognitive abilities such as logic, reasoning, and problem-solving, emotional intelligence focuses on our capacity to navigate the emotional landscape of life. It is the foundation of how we perceive ourselves, relate to others, and make decisions based on emotional information.

The Four Pillars of Emotional Intelligence

Emotional intelligence is built upon four key components: self-awareness, self-regulation, social awareness, and relationship management. Self-awareness involves the ability to recognize and understand our own emotions as they arise. It is about being in tune with our feelings, acknowledging them, and understanding their impact on our thoughts and actions. Self-regulation is the capacity to manage our emotions in healthy ways, to stay calm and composed under pressure, and to respond rather than react impulsively. Social awareness involves understanding the emotions of others, showing empathy, and being sensitive to social dynamics. Finally, relationship management is the ability to build and maintain healthy, positive relationships, to communicate effectively, and to manage conflicts constructively.

The Importance of Emotional Intelligence in Daily Life

Emotional intelligence plays a crucial role in every aspect of our lives. In our relationships, it allows us to connect more deeply with others, to communicate our needs and desires effectively, and to navigate conflicts with empathy and understanding. In the workplace, emotional intelligence is a key factor in leadership, teamwork, and collaboration. Leaders with high emotional intelligence can inspire and motivate their teams, create positive work environments, and make decisions that take into account the emotional well-being of their employees. Beyond personal and professional contexts, emotional intelligence also contributes to our overall well-being. It helps us manage stress, cope with challenges, and maintain a positive outlook on life.

The Role of Self-Awareness in Emotional Intelligence

Self-awareness is the cornerstone of emotional intelligence. Without it, the other components of emotional intelligence cannot be fully developed. Self-awareness involves a deep and honest understanding of our emotions, strengths, weaknesses, values, and motivations. It requires us to observe our thoughts and feelings without judgment, to recognize patterns in our behavior, and to understand how our emotions influence our actions and decisions. Through self-awareness, we gain insight into our emotional triggers and learn how to manage them effectively. We become more attuned to our needs and are better equipped to make choices that align with our values and long-term goals.

Developing Emotional Intelligence through Mindfulness

Mindfulness is a powerful tool for developing emotional intelligence. By practicing mindfulness, we learn to observe our emotions without becoming overwhelmed by them. We cultivate a non-judgmental awareness of our thoughts and feelings, allowing us to respond to situations with greater clarity and compassion. Mindfulness helps us stay present in the moment, reducing stress and enhancing our ability to manage our emotions. It also deepens our empathy and understanding of others, strengthening our social awareness and relationship management skills. As we integrate mindfulness into our daily lives, we naturally enhance our emotional intelligence, leading to more balanced, fulfilling relationships and a greater sense of inner peace.

1.1 The Foundations of Emotional Intelligence

Defining Emotional Intelligence

Emotional intelligence (EI) is the ability to perceive, understand, manage, and regulate emotions—both within ourselves and in others. Unlike cognitive intelligence, which is often measured through IQ tests and is primarily concerned with logical reasoning and problem-solving, emotional intelligence deals with the emotional aspects of human interaction. It encompasses a broad range of skills and behaviors that enable individuals to navigate social complexities, build stronger relationships, and make informed decisions that consider both emotional and rational factors. Understanding emotional intelligence begins with recognizing that emotions are a vital part of human experience, influencing how we think, act, and connect with others.

Historical Context and Evolution

The concept of emotional intelligence is relatively modern, though its roots can be traced back to early philosophical and psychological theories about emotions and behavior. The term "emotional intelligence" was popularized by psychologists Peter Salovey and John D. Mayer in the early 1990s, who defined it as a set of skills that contribute to accurate reasoning about emotions and the ability to use emotions to enhance thought. However, it was Daniel Goleman's groundbreaking work in 1995, particularly his book "Emotional Intelligence: Why It Can Matter More Than IQ," that brought the concept to mainstream attention. Goleman expanded on Salovey and Mayer's ideas, proposing that emotional intelligence was a crucial factor in personal and professional success, often more so than traditional IQ.

The Core Components of Emotional Intelligence

Emotional intelligence is built on several core components that interact to create a comprehensive framework for understanding and managing emotions. These components include self-awareness, self-regulation, motivation, empathy, and social skills. Self-awareness is the ability to recognize and understand one's own emotions, leading to a deeper understanding of how these emotions affect thoughts and behavior. Self-regulation involves managing one's emotional reactions, maintaining control over impulses, and adapting to changing circumstances. Motivation refers to the internal drive to achieve goals, often fueled by a deep-seated sense of purpose and optimism. Empathy is the capacity to understand and share the feelings of others, fostering deeper connections and more effective communication. Social skills encompass a wide range of abilities, including communication, conflict resolution, and relationship management, all of which are essential for successful interpersonal interactions.

The Interplay between Emotions and Cognition

Understanding emotional intelligence requires an appreciation of the intricate relationship between emotions and cognition. Emotions are not isolated from our thoughts; rather, they influence and are influenced by the way we perceive and process information. Cognitive processes, such as memory, attention, and decision-making, are often intertwined with emotional responses. For instance, a strong emotional reaction can color our perception of a situation, shaping our judgments and choices. Conversely, our thoughts and beliefs can trigger emotional responses, creating a feedback loop that can either enhance or impair our ability to think clearly and act rationally. Emotional intelligence involves recognizing this interplay and learning to manage it effectively, ensuring that our emotions serve as guides rather than obstacles in our cognitive processes.

The Role of Emotional Intelligence in Personal Development

Emotional intelligence plays a pivotal role in personal development, influencing our ability to grow, adapt, and thrive in various aspects of life. It contributes to greater self-understanding, allowing us to identify and work on areas that need improvement. By enhancing our emotional intelligence, we can develop healthier coping mechanisms, improve our resilience in the face of adversity, and cultivate a more positive outlook on life. Moreover, emotional intelligence is crucial in fostering self-compassion and empathy, enabling us to build stronger, more meaningful relationships with others. As we deepen our understanding of emotional intelligence and its foundations, we lay the groundwork for personal growth and a more fulfilling life.

1.2 The Role of Emotions in Our Lives

Understanding the Nature of Emotions

Emotions are fundamental to the human experience, influencing how we perceive and interact with the world around us. They are complex psychological states that encompass a range of feelings, thoughts, and behaviors. Emotions can be triggered by both internal and external stimuli, such as thoughts, memories, interactions with others, and environmental factors. At their core, emotions serve as signals that provide information about our internal states and the external environment. They are not random or irrational occurrences but rather meaningful responses that guide our actions and decisions. Understanding the nature of emotions is key to appreciating their role in shaping our lives and behaviors.

The Evolutionary Purpose of Emotions

From an evolutionary perspective, emotions have played a critical role in survival and adaptation. Early humans relied on emotions to navigate their environments, form social bonds, and respond to threats. For example, fear triggered the fight-or-flight response, which prepared individuals to either confront or escape danger. Joy and affection facilitated social bonding and cooperation, which were essential for the survival of early human communities. Even today, emotions continue to serve important functions, helping us to assess situations, communicate with others, and make decisions that enhance our well-being. By recognizing the evolutionary purpose of emotions, we can better understand their significance in our modern lives.

Emotions as Drivers of Behavior

Emotions are powerful drivers of behavior, often motivating us to take action in response to our needs and desires. For instance, the emotion of anger may prompt us to address a perceived injustice, while sadness may lead us to seek comfort and support from others. Joy and excitement can inspire us to pursue our goals and take risks, while fear can cause us to avoid situations that we perceive as dangerous. Emotions can also influence our long-term behaviors, shaping our habits, attitudes, and even our personality traits. By understanding how emotions drive behavior, we can learn to harness their power in constructive ways, channeling them toward positive outcomes.

The Social Function of Emotions

Emotions play a crucial role in our social interactions, serving as a means of communication and connection with others. Through facial expressions, body language, and vocal tone, we convey our emotional states to those around us, often without even realizing it. These nonverbal cues help to build rapport, foster empathy, and facilitate understanding in our relationships. Emotions also serve as social signals that guide our interactions with others. For example, expressions of happiness can strengthen bonds and encourage cooperation, while displays of anger can signal a need for boundary-setting or conflict resolution. By recognizing the social function of emotions, we can become more attuned to the emotional dynamics in our relationships and improve our ability to communicate effectively.

The Influence of Emotions on Decision-Making

Emotions play a significant role in the decision-making process, often guiding us in ways that are both conscious and unconscious. While we might like to think of ourselves as purely rational beings, the reality is that emotions frequently influence our choices. For example, a sense of anxiety might cause us to avoid taking a risk, even if the logical assessment of the situation suggests that the risk is minimal. On the other hand, a feeling of excitement or anticipation might encourage us to pursue an opportunity that we might otherwise overlook. Emotions can also serve as a form of intuitive wisdom, helping us to make decisions that align with our values and long-term goals. By understanding the influence of emotions on decision-making, we can become more mindful of how our feelings shape our choices and learn to make decisions that are both emotionally and logically sound.

Emotions and Well-Being

Emotions are deeply connected to our overall well-being, influencing our mental, emotional, and physical health. Positive emotions, such as joy, gratitude, and love, contribute to a sense of happiness and fulfillment, while negative emotions, such as anger, fear, and sadness, can lead to stress and discomfort. However, all emotions have value, and even negative emotions can serve important purposes, such as signaling the need for change or prompting us to address underlying issues. By cultivating emotional intelligence, we can learn to manage our emotions in ways that support our well-being, allowing us to experience a greater sense of balance, peace, and fulfillment in our lives.

1.3 The Benefits of Developing Emotional Intelligence

Enhanced Self-Awareness

One of the primary benefits of developing emotional intelligence is enhanced self-awareness. When we cultivate emotional intelligence, we become more attuned to our own emotions, thoughts, and behaviors. This self-awareness allows us to better understand our emotional triggers, recognize patterns in our responses, and identify the underlying causes of our feelings. As we become more aware of our emotional states, we gain greater insight into how our emotions influence our decisions and actions. This heightened self-awareness empowers us to make more conscious choices, respond to situations more effectively, and live in alignment with our values and goals.

Improved Emotional Regulation

Developing emotional intelligence also leads to improved emotional regulation, which is the ability to manage and control our emotional responses. Emotional regulation involves recognizing when we are experiencing intense emotions and employing strategies to calm ourselves, maintain composure, and respond in a balanced manner. By enhancing our emotional intelligence, we learn to navigate difficult emotions such as anger, frustration, and anxiety with greater ease. Instead of reacting impulsively, we can pause, reflect, and choose a more constructive response. Improved emotional regulation not only helps us manage stress and maintain emotional stability but also strengthens our relationships and enhances our overall well-being.

Stronger Interpersonal Relationships

Another significant benefit of developing emotional intelligence is the ability to build and maintain stronger interpersonal relationships. Emotional intelligence enhances our ability to understand and empathize with others, which is essential for effective communication and collaboration. By being more attuned to the emotions of those around us, we can respond with greater sensitivity and support, fostering deeper connections and trust. Emotional intelligence also helps us navigate conflicts more effectively, as we are better equipped to understand different perspectives and find mutually beneficial solutions. Whether in personal or professional settings, emotional intelligence is a key factor in creating and sustaining healthy, fulfilling relationships.

Increased Empathy and Compassion

As we develop emotional intelligence, we also cultivate greater empathy and compassion for others. Empathy involves the ability to understand and share the feelings of another person, while compassion is the desire to alleviate their suffering. These qualities are central to emotional intelligence and are crucial for fostering meaningful connections with others. Increased empathy allows us to better understand the emotions and experiences of those around us, leading to more supportive and caring interactions. Compassion, on the other hand, motivates us to take action to help others, whether through offering emotional support, lending a helping hand, or simply being present in times of need. By developing emotional intelligence, we become more compassionate individuals, contributing to a more compassionate and empathetic society.

Enhanced Decision-Making Abilities

Developing emotional intelligence also enhances our decision-making abilities. Emotions play a significant role in the decision-making process, often guiding our choices in ways that are both conscious and unconscious. When we cultivate emotional intelligence, we become more aware of how our emotions influence our decisions and learn to balance emotional and rational considerations. This balance allows us to make more informed and thoughtful decisions that align with our values and long-term goals. Emotional intelligence also helps us to navigate complex and emotionally charged situations with greater clarity and confidence, enabling us to make decisions that are both effective and compassionate.

Greater Resilience and Stress Management

Another important benefit of emotional intelligence is the development of greater resilience and improved stress management. Emotional intelligence equips us with the tools to cope with challenges and setbacks more effectively, allowing us to bounce back from adversity with greater ease. By understanding and managing our emotions, we can reduce the impact of stress on our mental and physical health, maintaining a sense of balance and well-being even in difficult circumstances. Emotional intelligence also helps us to cultivate a positive outlook, enabling us to approach challenges with optimism and confidence. As a result, we become more resilient individuals, better able to navigate the ups and downs of life.

Increased Overall Well-Being

Ultimately, developing emotional intelligence leads to increased overall well-being. By becoming more self-aware, improving emotional regulation, strengthening our relationships, and enhancing our decision-making abilities, we create a more balanced and fulfilling life. Emotional intelligence allows us to navigate the complexities of our emotions and relationships with greater ease, leading to a deeper sense of inner peace and contentment. As we cultivate emotional intelligence, we not only improve our well-being but also contribute to the well-being of those around us, creating a more harmonious and compassionate world.

Chapter 2: The Power of Mindfulness in Emotional Intelligence

Understanding Mindfulness

Mindfulness is the practice of being fully present in the moment, with an open and non-judgmental awareness of our thoughts, emotions, and sensations. It is about paying attention to what is happening right now, rather than being caught up in past regrets or future worries. Mindfulness involves observing our experiences without trying to change or resist them, allowing us to connect with our inner selves in a deeper and more meaningful way. By cultivating mindfulness, we can become more aware of our emotional states and how they influence our thoughts and behaviors, which is essential for developing emotional intelligence.

Mindfulness as a Tool for Emotional Awareness

One of the key ways mindfulness enhances emotional intelligence is by increasing emotional awareness. When we practice mindfulness, we learn to observe our emotions as they arise, without becoming overwhelmed or reactive. This heightened awareness allows us to recognize subtle emotional shifts and understand the underlying causes of our feelings. By becoming more attuned to our emotions, we can identify patterns in our emotional responses and gain insight into how our emotions influence our decisions and actions. This deepened emotional awareness is a crucial component of emotional intelligence, as it enables us to make more informed and conscious choices in our lives.

Mindfulness and Emotional Regulation

Mindfulness also plays a significant role in improving emotional regulation, which is the ability to manage and control our emotional responses. When we practice mindfulness, we develop the ability to observe our emotions without immediately reacting to them. This creates a space between stimulus and response, allowing us to choose how we want to respond to a situation, rather than being driven by impulsive reactions. Mindfulness helps us to stay calm and composed in the face of strong emotions, reducing the likelihood of being overwhelmed by anger, anxiety, or frustration. As we strengthen our emotional regulation skills through mindfulness, we become more resilient and better equipped to handle life's challenges.

The Impact of Mindfulness on Empathy and Compassion

Mindfulness not only enhances our self-awareness and emotional regulation but also deepens our capacity for empathy and compassion. By practicing mindfulness, we become more present in our interactions with others, which allows us to fully engage with their experiences and emotions. This heightened presence fosters greater empathy, as we become more attuned to the feelings and needs of those around us. Mindfulness also encourages us to approach ourselves and others with a sense of kindness and non-judgment, which naturally leads to increased compassion. As we cultivate mindfulness, we develop a more compassionate and empathetic outlook, which is essential for building strong and meaningful relationships.

Mindfulness and Stress Reduction

Another powerful benefit of mindfulness is its ability to reduce stress and promote emotional well-being. Mindfulness helps us to stay grounded in the present moment, preventing us from getting caught up in negative thought patterns or worrying about the future. By bringing our attention back to the here and now, we can break free from the cycle of rumination and reduce the impact of stress on our mental and physical health. Mindfulness also helps us to develop a more balanced perspective on life's challenges, enabling us to approach difficulties with greater calm and resilience. As we practice mindfulness, we create a sense of inner peace and stability, which is crucial for maintaining emotional intelligence in the face of stress.

Integrating Mindfulness into Daily Life

To fully harness the power of mindfulness in developing emotional intelligence, it is important to integrate mindfulness practices into our daily lives. This can be done through formal practices such as meditation, as well as informal practices such as mindful breathing, mindful walking, or simply taking a few moments each day to pause and check in with ourselves. By making mindfulness a regular part of our routine, we can continuously cultivate self-awareness, emotional regulation, empathy, and stress resilience. As mindfulness becomes ingrained in our daily lives, we naturally enhance our emotional intelligence, leading to a more balanced, fulfilling, and emotionally intelligent way of living.

2.1 What is Mindfulness?

The Essence of Mindfulness

Mindfulness is the practice of paying full attention to the present moment with an attitude of openness, curiosity, and non-judgment. At its core, mindfulness is about being fully engaged in whatever is happening right now, whether it's an external event or an internal experience like a thought or emotion. Instead of allowing the mind to wander or get caught up in distractions, mindfulness encourages us to bring our awareness back to the present moment. This presence enables us to experience life more fully, as we are not lost in past regrets or future anxieties but are fully immersed in the here and now.

Origins and History of Mindfulness

Mindfulness has its roots in ancient meditation practices, particularly within Buddhist traditions, where it has been practiced for thousands of years as a path to spiritual enlightenment and inner peace. The concept of mindfulness, known as "sati" in Pali, one of the languages of early Buddhist texts, refers to a form of mental training that involves cultivating a deep, focused awareness. Over time, mindfulness practices spread across different cultures and religious traditions, each adapting the practice to their contexts. In the modern era, mindfulness has been secularized and integrated into various therapeutic and wellness practices, gaining popularity for its benefits in stress reduction, emotional regulation, and overall well-being.

Mindfulness as a State of Being

Mindfulness is often described as a state of being, where the mind is fully aware of what is happening in the present moment without getting lost in thoughts, distractions, or judgments. This state of being is characterized by a sense of calm and clarity, where we can observe our thoughts and emotions without becoming entangled in them. In this mindful state, we are not trying to change or control our experiences; instead, we are simply noticing them with a gentle and accepting attitude. This approach allows us to experience the present moment more fully and to respond to situations with greater wisdom and compassion.

The Practice of Mindfulness

The practice of mindfulness can take many forms, from formal meditation sessions to informal everyday activities. Formal mindfulness practices often involve sitting quietly and focusing on the breath, bodily sensations, or a particular object of attention. As thoughts and distractions arise, the practitioner gently brings their attention back to the present moment. This simple practice of repeatedly returning to the present helps to strengthen the mind's ability to stay focused and aware. Informal mindfulness practices, on the other hand, can be integrated into daily activities such as eating, walking, or even washing dishes. The key is to bring full attention to the activity at hand, notice the sensory experiences, and stay fully engaged in the moment.

Mindfulness and the Non-Judgmental Attitude

A crucial aspect of mindfulness is the non-judgmental attitude that accompanies it. When practicing mindfulness, we are encouraged to observe our thoughts, emotions, and sensations without labeling them as good or bad, right or wrong. This non-judgmental stance allows us to see things as they are, without the overlay of personal biases or preconceived notions. By letting go of judgments, we create space for acceptance and understanding, which can lead to greater emotional balance and inner peace. This aspect of mindfulness is particularly important when dealing with difficult emotions, as it helps us to approach our experiences with compassion rather than resistance.

The Benefits of Mindfulness

Mindfulness offers a wide range of benefits that extend to various aspects of life, including mental, emotional, and physical well-being. Research has shown that mindfulness can reduce stress, improve focus, enhance emotional regulation, and increase overall life satisfaction. By helping us to stay present and aware, mindfulness enables us to respond to life's challenges with greater calm and resilience. Moreover, mindfulness fosters a deeper connection with ourselves and others, enhancing our relationships and contributing to a greater sense of fulfillment. As we continue to explore mindfulness, it becomes clear that this practice is not just about achieving a state of calm, but about cultivating a way of being that brings more awareness, compassion, and presence into our daily lives.

Mindfulness in the Modern World

In today's fast-paced and often chaotic world, mindfulness has become an increasingly valuable tool for navigating the complexities of modern life. With the constant demands on our attention from technology, work, and social obligations, it can be easy to feel overwhelmed and disconnected from the present moment. Mindfulness offers a way to reclaim our attention and bring more intention and awareness to our lives. Whether through formal meditation or simply taking a few moments to breathe deeply and center ourselves, mindfulness provides a refuge from the stress and distractions of everyday life, helping us to live with more clarity, balance, and purpose.

2.2 How Mindfulness Enhances Emotional Awareness

The Connection between Mindfulness and Emotional Awareness

Mindfulness is a powerful tool for enhancing emotional awareness, which is the ability to recognize and understand our emotions as they arise. By cultivating a mindful state, we become more attuned to our inner experiences, allowing us to observe our emotions without getting swept away by them. This connection between mindfulness and emotional awareness is fundamental to developing a deeper understanding of our emotional landscape. Through consistent mindfulness practice, we can learn to identify our emotions more accurately, recognize the triggers that cause them, and understand how they influence our thoughts, behaviors, and overall well-being.

Observing Emotions without Judgment

One of the key ways mindfulness enhances emotional awareness is by encouraging us to observe our emotions without judgment. When practicing mindfulness, we are taught to notice our feelings as they arise, without labeling them as good or bad. This non-judgmental observation allows us to see our emotions more clearly, without the distortions that often come from attaching value judgments. By removing these judgments, we can explore our emotions with curiosity and openness, leading to a greater understanding of their origins and effects. This approach also helps to reduce the intensity of negative emotions, as we are less likely to react impulsively or get caught in cycles of rumination.

Recognizing Emotional Triggers

Mindfulness also enhances emotional awareness by helping us to recognize the triggers that lead to certain emotional responses. As we practice mindfulness, we become more aware of the situations, thoughts, or physical sensations that precede our emotional reactions. This heightened awareness allows us to identify patterns in our emotional experiences, helping us to understand why certain situations provoke strong feelings. For example, we might notice that stress at work often leads to feelings of anxiety or frustration, or that certain memories trigger sadness or anger. By recognizing these triggers, we can better prepare ourselves to respond in a more balanced and thoughtful manner, rather than reacting automatically.

Understanding the Physical Manifestations of Emotions

Emotions are not just mental experiences; they are also closely tied to physical sensations in the body. Mindfulness helps us to become more aware of the physical manifestations of our emotions, such as tension in the shoulders, a racing heart, or a tightness in the chest. By paying attention to these bodily sensations, we can gain a deeper understanding of how our emotions are affecting us on a physical level. This awareness can be particularly helpful in managing stress and anxiety, as it allows us to recognize when our bodies are reacting to emotional stimuli and to take steps to calm ourselves. By connecting our emotional and physical experiences, mindfulness helps us to achieve a more holistic understanding of our emotional states.

Enhancing Emotional Vocabulary

Another way mindfulness enhances emotional awareness is by expanding our emotional vocabulary. As we become more mindful of our emotions, we learn to describe them with greater specificity and nuance. Instead of simply labeling our feelings as "good" or "bad," we might begin to recognize more subtle emotions, such as disappointment, contentment, or apprehension. This expanded emotional vocabulary allows us to articulate our experiences more accurately, both to ourselves and to others. By naming our emotions with precision, we can better understand the complexities of our emotional landscape and communicate our feelings in a way that fosters understanding and connection with others.

Creating Space between Emotion and Reaction

Mindfulness creates a crucial space between the experience of an emotion and our reaction to it. In this space, we have the opportunity to observe our emotions without immediately acting on them. This pause allows us to choose how we want to respond, rather than reacting impulsively or habitually. For example, instead of lashing out in anger when provoked, we might notice the anger arising, take a moment to breathe, and then respond in a way that aligns with our values and long-term goals. This ability to create space between emotion and reaction is a key component of emotional intelligence and is fostered through regular mindfulness practice.

The Ongoing Practice of Emotional Awareness

Enhancing emotional awareness through mindfulness is an ongoing process that requires regular practice and reflection. As we continue to cultivate mindfulness, we deepen our understanding of our emotional experiences and develop greater control over our responses. Over time, this practice leads to a more balanced and emotionally intelligent way of living, where we are more in tune with our inner selves and better equipped to navigate the complexities of our emotional world. By integrating mindfulness into our daily lives, we can continue to enhance our emotional awareness, leading to greater self-understanding, improved relationships, and a more fulfilling life.

2.3 The Connection between Mindfulness and Emotional Regulation

Understanding Emotional Regulation

Emotional regulation is the ability to manage and respond to emotional experiences in a balanced and constructive way. It involves recognizing emotions as they arise, understanding their impact, and choosing how to express or act upon them. Effective emotional regulation allows individuals to maintain emotional stability, even in challenging situations, and prevents emotions from overwhelming their thoughts or actions. It is a crucial aspect of emotional intelligence and plays a significant role in mental well-being, relationships, and overall life satisfaction.

Mindfulness as a Pathway to Emotional Regulation

Mindfulness serves as a powerful tool for enhancing emotional regulation by promoting a state of awareness and acceptance. When we practice mindfulness, we learn to observe our emotions without immediately reacting to them. This practice helps us create a mental space between the experience of an emotion and our response, allowing us to choose a more measured and intentional reaction. By cultivating this awareness, mindfulness enables us to regulate our emotions more effectively, preventing impulsive or destructive behaviors and fostering a greater sense of emotional balance.

The Role of Mindful Observation in Emotional Regulation

One of the key ways mindfulness aids in emotional regulation is through mindful observation. Mindful observation involves paying close attention to our emotions as they arise, without trying to suppress or amplify them. By observing emotions with curiosity and non-judgment, we can gain insights into their underlying causes and the patterns they follow. This practice helps us to understand our emotional triggers and the situations that lead to strong emotional reactions. With this understanding, we can anticipate and manage our emotional responses more effectively, choosing strategies that promote emotional well-being rather than reacting impulsively.

Mindfulness and the Ability to Pause Before Reacting

Mindfulness encourages the practice of pausing before reacting to emotional stimuli. This pause is a critical component of emotional regulation, as it allows us to step back from our immediate emotional response and consider the most appropriate course of action. For instance, when we feel anger rising in response to a perceived slight, mindfulness enables us to pause, take a deep breath, and reflect on the situation before reacting. This moment of pause allows us to respond in a way that aligns with our values and long-term goals, rather than being driven by the intensity of the emotion. Over time, this practice strengthens our ability to regulate emotions in various situations.

Reducing Emotional Reactivity through Mindfulness

Emotional reactivity refers to the tendency to respond quickly and intensely to emotional stimuli, often without full awareness of the consequences. Mindfulness helps to reduce emotional reactivity by promoting a calm and centered state of mind. Through mindfulness practice, we learn to stay grounded in the present moment, even when faced with challenging emotions. This groundedness reduces the likelihood of being swept away by emotions, allowing us to respond with greater clarity and composure. As a result, mindfulness helps to decrease the frequency and intensity of emotionally reactive behaviors, leading to more thoughtful and deliberate responses.

Mindfulness and the Acceptance of Emotions

Another important aspect of mindfulness in emotional regulation is the acceptance of emotions. Mindfulness teaches us to accept our emotions as they are, without trying to change or resist them. This acceptance allows us to experience emotions fully without becoming overwhelmed by them. By accepting our emotions, we can process them more effectively and healthily move through them. This approach contrasts with the common tendency to suppress or avoid uncomfortable emotions, which can lead to increased emotional distress over time. Mindfulness fosters a healthy relationship with our emotions, where we acknowledge and honor them without letting them control us.

Building Resilience through Mindful Emotional Regulation

Mindfulness also contributes to building emotional resilience, the capacity to recover quickly from emotional challenges. By practicing mindfulness, we develop the skills needed to navigate difficult emotions with greater ease and confidence. Mindfulness helps us to remain calm and centered in the face of emotional turmoil, reducing the impact of stress and allowing us to bounce back more quickly. This resilience is crucial for maintaining emotional health and well-being, particularly in the face of life's inevitable ups and downs. Through mindful emotional regulation, we build the inner strength needed to handle adversity with grace and maintain emotional equilibrium.

Integrating Mindfulness into Daily Emotional Regulation

To fully benefit from the connection between mindfulness and emotional regulation, it is essential to integrate mindfulness practices into daily life. This can involve setting aside time for formal mindfulness meditation, as well as incorporating mindful moments throughout the day. For example, taking a few deep breaths before responding to a stressful email, or practicing mindful walking during a break, can reinforce the habit of emotional regulation. By consistently practicing mindfulness, we can enhance our ability to manage emotions effectively, leading to a more balanced and fulfilling life.

Chapter 3: Cultivating Self-Awareness through Mindfulness

The Importance of Self-Awareness

Self-awareness is the ability to recognize and understand our thoughts, emotions, and behaviors. It involves a deep and honest reflection on who we are, how we think, and how we react to various situations. Self-awareness is crucial for personal growth, as it enables us to identify our strengths and weaknesses, understand our values and beliefs, and recognize the impact of our actions on ourselves and others. By cultivating self-awareness, we can make more informed choices, improve our relationships, and lead a more authentic and fulfilling life.

Mindfulness as a Tool for Self-Discovery

Mindfulness is a powerful tool for cultivating self-awareness because it encourages us to turn our attention inward and observe our inner experiences with clarity and curiosity. Through mindfulness, we learn to become more attuned to our thoughts, emotions, and physical sensations, noticing patterns and tendencies that we might otherwise overlook. This practice of self-observation allows us to gain deeper insights into our inner world, helping us to understand the motivations behind our actions and the factors that influence our decision-making processes. As we continue to practice mindfulness, we develop a more nuanced understanding of ourselves, which is the foundation for true self-awareness.

Observing Thoughts and Beliefs

One of the key aspects of cultivating self-awareness through mindfulness is observing our thoughts and beliefs. Our thoughts are constantly shaping our perceptions of the world and influencing our emotions and actions. By practicing mindfulness, we can observe these thoughts as they arise, without becoming entangled in them. This observation allows us to identify recurring thought patterns, such as negative self-talk or limiting beliefs, that may be holding us back. Through mindful observation, we can begin to challenge and reframe these thoughts, leading to a more positive and empowering mindset. This process of observing and reflecting on our thoughts is essential for developing a deeper understanding of our mental landscape.

Exploring Emotional Responses

Mindfulness also enhances self-awareness by helping us to explore our emotional responses in a non-judgmental way. Emotions are powerful forces that influence our behavior and decision-making, often without our conscious awareness. By practicing mindfulness, we learn to recognize our emotions as they arise and to observe them without immediately reacting. This mindful exploration of our emotions allows us to understand the underlying causes of our emotional responses and to see how they influence our interactions with others. As we become more aware of our emotional triggers and patterns, we can develop greater emotional intelligence and learn to respond to situations in a more balanced and thoughtful way.

Becoming Aware of Physical Sensations

In addition to thoughts and emotions, mindfulness also helps us to become more aware of our physical sensations. Our bodies often hold clues to our emotional and mental states, such as tension in the shoulders indicating stress or a racing heart signaling anxiety. By practicing mindfulness, we can tune into these physical sensations and gain a deeper understanding of how our bodies are responding to different situations. This awareness allows us to take better care of our physical and emotional health, as we can recognize when we need to rest, relax, or address underlying issues. Mindfulness helps us to listen to our bodies and to cultivate a more holistic sense of self-awareness.

Mindfulness and the Acceptance of Self

A key component of self-awareness is the acceptance of oneself, including both strengths and weaknesses. Mindfulness fosters self-acceptance by encouraging us to observe our inner experiences without judgment. As we practice mindfulness, we learn to accept our thoughts, emotions, and physical sensations as they are, without trying to change or suppress them. This acceptance creates a sense of inner peace and allows us to embrace our true selves, including our imperfections. By cultivating self-acceptance, we can let go of the need for constant self-improvement and instead focus on living authentically and in alignment with our values.

The Continuous Journey of Self-Awareness

Cultivating self-awareness through mindfulness is an ongoing journey that requires consistent practice and reflection. As we continue to practice mindfulness, we deepen our understanding of ourselves and develop greater clarity about our values, motivations, and goals. This continuous journey of self-discovery allows us to live more intentionally and to make choices that are aligned with our true selves. By integrating mindfulness into our daily lives, we can continue to grow in self-awareness and lead a more authentic and fulfilling life.

Applying Self-Awareness in Everyday Life

The self-awareness cultivated through mindfulness is not just an abstract concept; it has practical applications in everyday life. By becoming more aware of our thoughts, emotions, and behaviors, we can make more conscious choices in our relationships, work, and personal life. Self-awareness helps us to communicate more effectively, to set healthy boundaries, and to navigate challenges with greater resilience. It also allows us to align our actions with our values and to live in a way that is true to ourselves. Through mindfulness, we can bring the insights gained from self-awareness into every aspect of our lives, leading to greater fulfillment and well-being.

3.1 Techniques for Mindful Self-Reflection

Journaling as a Tool for Self-Reflection

Journaling is a powerful technique for mindful self-reflection that allows us to capture and explore our thoughts, emotions, and experiences in writing. By regularly setting aside time to write about our day, our feelings, or our reactions to specific events, we can gain valuable insights into our inner world. The act of writing slows down the thought process, making it easier to notice patterns, identify emotional triggers, and explore underlying beliefs. Journaling also provides a safe space to express emotions without judgment, helping to clarify thoughts and uncover hidden aspects of ourselves. Over time, this practice deepens self-awareness and fosters personal growth, as it enables us to reflect on our actions and their consequences.

Mindful Breathing for Present-Moment Awareness

Mindful breathing is a simple yet effective technique for enhancing self-awareness by bringing attention to the present moment. This practice involves focusing on the breath as it flows in and out of the body, observing each inhale and exhale without trying to change the natural rhythm. By concentrating on the breath, we can quiet the mind and create a space for self-reflection. This focused attention helps us to become more aware of our thoughts and emotions as they arise, allowing us to observe them without becoming attached or overwhelmed. Mindful breathing can be practiced anywhere and at any time, making it a versatile tool for developing greater self-awareness and fostering a deeper connection with ourselves.

Body Scan Meditation for Physical and Emotional Awareness

The body scan meditation is a mindfulness technique that involves paying close attention to physical sensations in the body, from head to toe. By guiding our awareness through each part of the body, we can detect areas of tension, discomfort, or relaxation, and explore the emotions associated with these sensations. This practice helps to bridge the mind-body connection, revealing how emotions are stored and expressed physically. Through regular body scan meditation, we become more attuned to our body's signals, enabling us to respond to stress, anxiety, or other emotional states with greater awareness and care. This technique also promotes relaxation and emotional release, contributing to overall well-being.

Mindful Observation of Thoughts

Mindful observation of thoughts is a technique that involves watching our thoughts as they come and go, without getting caught up in their content. This practice helps us to develop a more detached perspective on our thinking patterns, allowing us to see thoughts as transient mental events rather than absolute truths. By observing thoughts mindfully, we can identify recurring themes, such as self-criticism, worry, or negativity, and explore how these patterns influence our emotions and behavior. This technique fosters greater self-awareness by revealing the automatic thoughts that often drive our actions. With practice, mindful observation of thoughts can help us to break free from unhelpful thought patterns and cultivate a more balanced and positive mindset.

Engaging in Mindful Walking

Mindful walking is a dynamic form of meditation that combines movement with mindfulness, encouraging self-reflection through the simple act of walking. This practice involves paying attention to the sensations of each step, the movement of the body, and the environment around us. As we walk mindfully, we become more aware of our physical presence, our thoughts, and our emotional state. This practice allows us to reflect on our inner experiences in a natural and relaxed way, often leading to new insights and a deeper connection with ourselves. Mindful walking can be particularly effective for those who find sitting meditation challenging, as it integrates mindfulness into everyday activities, making self-reflection more accessible.

Practicing Loving-Kindness Meditation

Loving-kindness meditation is a mindfulness practice that focuses on cultivating feelings of compassion and kindness towards ourselves and others. This technique involves silently repeating phrases such as "May I be happy, may I be healthy, may I be safe" while directing these intentions towards oneself and others. By practicing loving-kindness meditation, we can develop a more compassionate and accepting attitude toward ourselves, which is essential for meaningful self-reflection. This practice helps to soften self-criticism and judgment, creating a supportive inner environment where we can explore our thoughts and emotions with greater openness and understanding. Loving-kindness meditation also strengthens the connection between self-awareness and empathy, enhancing our ability to relate to ourselves and others with kindness.

Incorporating Self-Reflection into Daily Life

To fully benefit from these techniques, it is essential to integrate mindful self-reflection into daily life. This can be done by setting aside dedicated time each day for practices like journaling, meditation, or mindful walking. Additionally, self-reflection can be woven into routine activities, such as taking a few mindful breaths before starting the day or reflecting on emotions while waiting in line. The key is to make self-reflection a regular part of life, rather than a sporadic activity. By consistently engaging in mindful self-reflection, we can deepen our self-awareness, gain valuable insights into our thoughts and emotions, and ultimately lead a more intentional and fulfilling life.

3.2 Recognizing and Understanding Your Emotions

The Importance of Emotional Awareness

Recognizing and understanding your emotions is a fundamental aspect of emotional intelligence. Emotions influence every aspect of our lives, from decision-making and relationships to overall well-being. Developing emotional awareness allows us to identify and acknowledge our feelings as they arise, rather than ignoring or suppressing them. By becoming more attuned to our emotional states, we can better understand the underlying causes of our feelings and respond to them in healthier, more constructive ways. This awareness is crucial for self-reflection, as it provides insight into how emotions shape our thoughts, behaviors, and interactions with others.

Identifying Different Emotions

One of the first steps in recognizing and understanding your emotions is learning to identify them accurately. Emotions can be complex and multifaceted, often involving a mix of different feelings that can be difficult to distinguish. By paying close attention to our emotional experiences, we can begin to label our emotions more precisely. For example, rather than simply feeling "bad," we might recognize that we are experiencing sadness, frustration, or anxiety. By refining our emotional vocabulary, we can better articulate what we are feeling and gain a clearer understanding of our emotional landscape. This process of identifying emotions also helps to prevent misunderstandings in communication, as it allows us to express our feelings more accurately to others.

Understanding the Causes of Emotions

Once we have identified our emotions, the next step is to understand their underlying causes. Emotions are often triggered by specific events, thoughts, or memories, and recognizing these triggers is essential for emotional awareness. By reflecting on the circumstances that led to a particular emotional response, we can uncover the root causes of our feelings. This understanding helps us to make sense of our emotions and provides context for why we react in certain ways. For example, if we feel anger in a particular situation, examining the cause might reveal that we feel disrespected or misunderstood. By identifying these triggers, we can take steps to address the underlying issues and manage our emotional responses more effectively.

Exploring the Intensity of Emotions

In addition to identifying and understanding the causes of our emotions, it is also important to explore the intensity of our feelings. Emotions can vary in strength, from mild irritation to overwhelming rage, and recognizing this intensity is key to managing our emotional responses. By assessing how strongly we feel about a particular situation, we can determine whether our reaction is proportionate to the event or if it is being influenced by other factors, such as past experiences or unresolved issues. Understanding the intensity of our emotions allows us to respond more appropriately and avoid overreacting or underreacting to situations. It also helps us to develop greater emotional resilience, as we learn to navigate both strong and subtle emotional experiences with greater ease.

Connecting Emotions to Physical Sensations

Emotions are not just mental experiences; they also have a physical component. Our bodies often reflect our emotional states through physical sensations, such as a racing heart when anxious or tight shoulders when stressed. By paying attention to these physical cues, we can gain additional insight into our emotions and how they manifest in the body. This awareness helps us to recognize emotions more quickly, even before they fully register in our conscious mind. For example, noticing a tightness in the chest might signal the onset of anxiety, allowing us to take steps to manage it before it escalates. By connecting our emotions to physical sensations, we can develop a more holistic understanding of our emotional experiences and learn to respond to them more effectively.

The Role of Self-Compassion in Emotional Understanding

Recognizing and understanding our emotions also involves practicing self-compassion. Emotions, especially difficult ones, can be challenging to confront, and it is important to approach them with kindness and understanding. Self-compassion allows us to accept our emotions without judgment, recognizing that it is normal to experience a wide range of feelings. By being gentle with ourselves when we encounter difficult emotions, we create a supportive environment where we can explore and understand our feelings more deeply. This compassionate approach also helps to reduce the tendency to suppress or deny emotions, which can lead to greater emotional distress in the long run. Self-compassion fosters a healthier relationship with our emotions, enabling us to navigate them with greater ease and resilience.

Applying Emotional Awareness in Daily Life

Recognizing and understanding our emotions is not just an abstract exercise; it has practical applications in everyday life. By developing emotional awareness, we can make more informed decisions, communicate more effectively, and build stronger relationships. For example, being aware of our emotions can help us to choose words that accurately convey our feelings during a difficult conversation, leading to better understanding and resolution. Similarly, understanding the causes and intensity of our emotions can help us to manage stress, prevent burnout, and maintain emotional balance in challenging situations. By applying emotional awareness in daily life, we can enhance our overall well-being and lead a more emotionally fulfilling life.

3.3 The Impact of Self-Awareness on Emotional Intelligence

The Foundation of Emotional Intelligence

Self-awareness is the cornerstone of emotional intelligence, serving as the foundation upon which other aspects of emotional intelligence are built. Without self-awareness, it is difficult to develop the other key components of emotional intelligence, such as self-regulation, empathy, and social skills. Self-awareness involves a deep understanding of one's emotions, motivations, strengths, and weaknesses. This understanding enables us to recognize how our emotions influence our behavior and how our actions affect others. By cultivating self-awareness, we lay the groundwork for improving our emotional intelligence, as it allows us to approach our emotions and interactions with greater clarity and intentionality.

Enhancing Emotional Regulation through Self-Awareness

One of the most significant impacts of self-awareness on emotional intelligence is its role in enhancing emotional regulation. Emotional regulation refers to our ability to manage and respond to our emotions healthily and constructively. When we are self-aware, we can identify our emotional triggers and recognize when our emotions are starting to escalate. This awareness allows us to intervene before our emotions get out of control, allowing us to choose how we want to respond. For example, if we notice that we are becoming angry, self-awareness can help us take a step back, breathe, and approach the situation with a calm and measured response. By improving our ability to regulate our emotions, self-awareness helps us to maintain emotional balance and avoid impulsive or reactive behavior.

Strengthening Empathy through Self-Awareness

Self-awareness also plays a crucial role in strengthening empathy, which is the ability to understand and share the feelings of others. When we are in tune with our own emotions, we become more attuned to the emotions of others. Self-awareness allows us to recognize the similarities between our emotional experiences and those of others, fostering a deeper sense of connection and understanding. By understanding our emotional responses, we can better interpret and respond to the emotions of others, leading to more empathetic and compassionate interactions. This heightened empathy not only improves our relationships but also enhances our ability to navigate social situations with sensitivity and insight.

Improving Decision-Making and Problem-Solving

Another key impact of self-awareness on emotional intelligence is its ability to improve decision-making and problem-solving skills. Emotions play a significant role in the decisions we make, often influencing our choices in ways we may not fully realize. When we are self-aware, we can recognize how our emotions are affecting our judgment and take steps to ensure that our decisions are informed by both rational thought and emotional insight. For example, if we are feeling anxious about a decision, self-awareness allows us to acknowledge that anxiety and assess whether it is based on valid concerns or irrational fears. This balanced approach to decision-making leads to more thoughtful and effective problem-solving, as we are better able to weigh the emotional and logical aspects of a situation.

Building Stronger Relationships through Self-Awareness

Self-awareness has a profound impact on our relationships, as it enhances our ability to communicate effectively and build trust with others. When we are aware of our own emotions, we can express our feelings more clearly and authentically, which leads to more honest and open communication. This transparency fosters trust and strengthens the bonds we share with others. Additionally, self-awareness helps us to recognize the impact of our behavior on others, allowing us to adjust our actions to create more positive and supportive interactions. For example, if we notice that we tend to become defensive in certain situations, self-awareness can help us to take a step back and respond more calmly, leading to healthier and more constructive relationships.

Fostering Personal Growth and Development

Finally, self-awareness is a key driver of personal growth and development, which is an essential component of emotional intelligence. By regularly reflecting on our thoughts, emotions, and behaviors, we can identify areas for improvement and take proactive steps to grow and evolve. Self-awareness encourages us to confront our weaknesses and challenges, while also recognizing and celebrating our strengths. This continuous process of self-examination and growth leads to greater self-confidence and resilience, as we develop a deeper understanding of who we are and what we are capable of achieving. By fostering personal growth, self-awareness helps us to become more emotionally intelligent individuals who are better equipped to navigate the complexities of life.

Integrating Self-Awareness into Everyday Life

The impact of self-awareness on emotional intelligence is most profound when it is integrated into everyday life. This can be achieved by regularly practicing mindfulness, journaling, or engaging in self-reflection exercises that promote greater self-understanding. By making self-awareness a daily habit, we can continuously improve our emotional intelligence and enhance our ability to navigate the emotional landscape of our lives. This integration not only benefits our well-being but also positively influences our interactions with others, leading to more meaningful and fulfilling relationships. Ultimately, self-awareness is the key to unlocking the full potential of our emotional intelligence, allowing us to live more intentional, balanced, and emotionally intelligent lives.

Chapter 4: Practicing Emotional Regulation with Mindfulness

Understanding Emotional Regulation

Emotional regulation is the process of managing and responding to our emotions in a way that is constructive and appropriate to the situation. It involves recognizing our emotional responses, understanding their underlying causes, and choosing how to express or modulate them. Effective emotional regulation allows us to navigate challenging situations with greater ease, maintain emotional balance, and avoid impulsive reactions that may lead to negative outcomes. By practicing emotional regulation, we can create a sense of inner stability and resilience, which is essential for overall well-being. Mindfulness, with its focus on present-moment awareness and non-judgmental observation, is a powerful tool for enhancing emotional regulation.

The Role of Mindfulness in Emotional Regulation

Mindfulness plays a crucial role in emotional regulation by helping us develop greater awareness of our emotional states and the factors that influence them. Through mindfulness practices, such as meditation, breathing exercises, and mindful observation, we can learn to observe our emotions without immediately reacting to them. This pause between feeling and action provides the space needed to choose how we want to respond, rather than being driven by automatic emotional impulses. Mindfulness also helps to reduce the intensity of difficult emotions, as it encourages us to approach them with curiosity and acceptance, rather than resistance or avoidance. By integrating mindfulness into our daily lives, we can cultivate a more balanced and mindful approach to emotional regulation.

Identifying Emotional Triggers with Mindfulness

One of the key aspects of practicing emotional regulation with mindfulness is the ability to identify emotional triggers. Emotional triggers are specific situations, thoughts, or memories that elicit strong emotional reactions, often without our conscious awareness. By practicing mindfulness, we can become more attuned to these triggers and recognize them as they arise. For example, through mindful observation, we might notice that certain types of criticism consistently lead to feelings of anger or defensiveness. By identifying these triggers, we can prepare ourselves to respond more calmly and thoughtfully when they occur. Mindfulness helps us to create a mental map of our emotional landscape, allowing us to navigate it with greater awareness and control.

Using Mindful Breathing to Calm Emotional Responses

Mindful breathing is an effective technique for calming emotional responses and regulating emotions in the moment. When we experience strong emotions, such as anger, anxiety, or frustration, our body's stress response is activated, leading to physical symptoms like rapid heartbeat, shallow breathing, and muscle tension. By practicing mindful breathing, we can slow down our breath, which in turn signals to the body that it is safe to relax. This physiological shift helps to reduce the intensity of the emotional response, making it easier to manage. Mindful breathing also brings our attention back to the present moment, allowing us to step out of the emotional narrative and approach the situation with a clearer, more balanced perspective.

Practicing Non-Judgmental Awareness of Emotions

A core principle of mindfulness is the practice of non-judgmental awareness, which involves observing our thoughts and emotions without labeling them as good or bad. This approach is particularly beneficial for emotional regulation, as it encourages us to accept our emotions as they are, rather than trying to suppress or change them. By observing our emotions with non-judgmental awareness, we can gain insight into their nature and the messages they carry, without becoming overwhelmed or reactive. This practice allows us to maintain a sense of equanimity, even in the face of challenging emotions. Over time, non-judgmental awareness helps to reduce the power that difficult emotions have over us, making it easier to regulate them.

Creating a Mindful Response Plan

To effectively practice emotional regulation with mindfulness, it can be helpful to create a mindful response plan. This plan involves identifying the emotions that you find most challenging to regulate and developing specific mindfulness techniques to address them. For example, if you struggle with anxiety, your response plan might include practicing mindful breathing or grounding exercises whenever you feel anxious. If anger is a challenge, you might plan to take a mindful pause and reflect on the situation before responding. By having a mindful response plan in place, you can approach emotional regulation with greater intention and preparedness, rather than reacting impulsively. This plan can be adjusted over time as you gain more experience with mindfulness and emotional regulation.

Integrating Mindfulness into Daily Life for Emotional Regulation

The benefits of practicing emotional regulation with mindfulness are most profound when mindfulness is integrated into daily life. This can be achieved by setting aside time each day for formal mindfulness practices, such as meditation or mindful breathing, as well as incorporating mindfulness into routine activities, like eating, walking, or working. By consistently engaging in mindfulness, you can strengthen your ability to regulate emotions in real time, regardless of the situation. The key is to make mindfulness a regular part of your life, rather than a sporadic activity. With practice, mindfulness becomes a natural way of being, allowing you to navigate your emotions with greater ease, balance, and resilience.

The Long-Term Impact of Mindful Emotional Regulation

Practicing emotional regulation with mindfulness has a lasting impact on both emotional intelligence and overall well-being. Over time, it leads to greater emotional stability, improved relationships, and enhanced mental health. Mindful emotional regulation helps to break the cycle of reactive behavior, replacing it with thoughtful, intentional responses that align with your values and goals. This practice also fosters a deeper understanding of yourself and your emotions, leading to greater self-compassion and inner peace. As you continue to cultivate mindfulness in your life, you will find that emotional regulation becomes second nature, allowing you to approach life's challenges with a calm, centered, and balanced mindset.

4.1 Mindful Breathing and Its Role in Emotional Balance

The Basics of Mindful Breathing

Mindful breathing is a simple yet powerful technique that involves focusing attention on the breath as it moves in and out of the body. This practice serves as a foundation for many mindfulness exercises, providing a steady anchor that helps bring awareness to the present moment. Unlike ordinary breathing, mindful breathing requires an intentional focus on each inhalation and exhalation, noticing the sensations of the breath without trying to control it. This focused awareness of the breath helps to quiet the mind, reduce distractions, and create a sense of calm. Mindful breathing is accessible to anyone and can be practiced anywhere, making it an ideal tool for cultivating emotional balance.

Regulating the Nervous System through Breath

One of the key benefits of mindful breathing is its ability to regulate the nervous system, which plays a crucial role in managing emotions. When we experience stress or strong emotions like anger or fear, our body's fight-or-flight response is activated, leading to physical symptoms such as rapid heartbeat, shallow breathing, and muscle tension. Mindful breathing counteracts this response by stimulating the parasympathetic nervous system, which promotes relaxation and reduces the stress response. By slowing down the breath and deepening each inhalation and exhalation, we send signals to the brain that it is safe to relax. This physiological shift helps to calm the mind and body, allowing us to regain emotional balance more quickly.

Enhancing Emotional Awareness through Breath

Mindful breathing also enhances emotional awareness by bringing our attention to the present moment and allowing us to observe our emotions without judgment. Often, our emotions can feel overwhelming because they are entangled with thoughts and narratives that amplify their intensity. By focusing on the breath, we create a mental space where we can observe our emotions more objectively. This practice helps us to distinguish between the actual emotion we are experiencing and the thoughts that may be fueling it. For example, during a moment of anxiety, mindful breathing can help us recognize the physical sensation of the emotion—such as a tight chest or fluttering stomach—without getting caught up in anxious thoughts. This heightened awareness of emotions as they arise is a crucial step in emotional regulation and balance.

Interrupting Negative Thought Patterns

Negative thought patterns often accompany strong emotions, leading to a cycle of rumination and emotional distress. Mindful breathing can serve as an effective tool for interrupting these patterns and redirecting attention to the present moment. When we focus on our breath, we are less likely to get caught up in repetitive or negative thinking. This break in the thought pattern allows us to step back from our emotions and see them in a new light. By consistently practicing mindful breathing, we can develop greater control over our mental focus and reduce the impact of negative thoughts on our emotional well-being. Over time, this practice helps to weaken the grip of unhelpful thought patterns, fostering a more balanced and resilient emotional state.

Creating a Mindful Breathing Routine

To fully experience the benefits of mindful breathing for emotional balance, it is important to establish a regular practice. This can be done by setting aside a few minutes each day to focus on your breath, whether through formal meditation or simply taking mindful breaths during everyday activities. For beginners, it can be helpful to start with short sessions of mindful breathing, gradually increasing the duration as comfort and familiarity with the practice grow. Consistency is key to reaping the long-term benefits, as regular practice helps to strengthen the mind's ability to focus and regulate emotions. By integrating mindful breathing into your daily routine, you create a reliable tool for maintaining emotional balance, regardless of external circumstances.

Applying Mindful Breathing in Challenging Situations

Mindful breathing is not only a practice for calm moments but also a powerful tool to use in challenging situations. When faced with stress, conflict, or overwhelming emotions, taking a few mindful breaths can help to center your mind and body, allowing you to respond more thoughtfully and calmly. For example, during a difficult conversation, pausing to take a deep, mindful breath can prevent reactive responses and create a moment of clarity. This brief pause allows you to choose how to respond, rather than being driven by emotion. By applying mindful breathing in real-time situations, you can maintain emotional balance even in the face of adversity.

The Long-Term Impact of Mindful Breathing on Emotional Health

The long-term impact of mindful breathing on emotional health is profound. Regular practice not only enhances immediate emotional balance but also builds emotional resilience over time. By consistently engaging in mindful breathing, you train your mind to remain calm and focused, even in the face of emotional turbulence. This resilience allows you to navigate life's challenges with greater ease and confidence, reducing the likelihood of being overwhelmed by stress or difficult emotions. Moreover, the practice of mindful breathing fosters a deeper connection between mind and body, promoting overall well-being and a sense of inner peace. As you continue to cultivate mindful breathing, you will find that emotional balance becomes a natural and enduring part of your daily life.

4.2 Techniques for Managing Stress and Anxiety

Understanding the Impact of Stress and Anxiety

Stress and anxiety are common experiences in today's fast-paced world, often triggered by work pressures, personal responsibilities, or uncertain situations. While both stress and anxiety serve as natural responses to perceived threats, prolonged exposure can lead to negative effects on mental and physical health. Chronic stress can contribute to conditions such as high blood pressure, heart disease, and a weakened immune system, while anxiety can lead to persistent worry, sleep disturbances, and emotional exhaustion. Understanding the impact of stress and anxiety is the first step in managing them effectively. By recognizing the signs and symptoms, we can take proactive steps to address these feelings before they escalate.

Mindful Breathing for Immediate Relief

Mindful breathing is one of the most accessible and effective techniques for managing stress and anxiety in the moment. When faced with a stressful situation or anxious thoughts, focusing on the breath can help calm the nervous system and bring the mind back to the present. One simple method is the 4-7-8 breathing technique, which involves inhaling through the nose for a count of four, holding the breath for a count of seven, and exhaling through the mouth for a count of eight. This practice helps to slow down the heart rate and promote relaxation. By regularly practicing mindful breathing, you can create a natural response to stress that helps to quickly reduce its intensity.

Progressive Muscle Relaxation for Physical Tension

Stress and anxiety often manifest as physical tension in the body, particularly in areas like the shoulders, neck, and jaw. Progressive muscle relaxation (PMR) is a technique that involves systematically tensing and then relaxing different muscle groups to release built-up tension. To practice PMR, start by focusing on one muscle group at a time, such as your feet, and gradually work your way up the body. Tense each muscle group for about five seconds, then release and notice the difference in how your body feels. This practice not only helps to alleviate physical tension but also promotes a deeper awareness of the connection between mind and body, making it easier to recognize and manage stress-related symptoms.

Mindfulness Meditation for Long-Term Stress Management

Mindfulness meditation is a powerful tool for long-term stress management, helping to reduce the overall levels of stress and anxiety by promoting a state of calm and presence. Unlike other forms of meditation, mindfulness meditation focuses on observing thoughts, emotions, and bodily sensations without judgment. By regularly practicing mindfulness meditation, you can train your mind to respond to stress and anxiety with greater awareness and equanimity. Start with short sessions of five to ten minutes and gradually increase the duration as you become more comfortable with the practice. Over time, mindfulness meditation can help to rewire the brain, making it less reactive to stressors and more resilient in the face of challenges.

Journaling as a Stress-Relief Tool

Journaling is an effective technique for managing stress and anxiety by providing an outlet for processing thoughts and emotions. Writing about stressful experiences or anxious thoughts can help to clarify what is causing these feelings and provide insight into how to address them. Additionally, journaling can serve as a way to track patterns in your stress and anxiety, allowing you to identify triggers and develop strategies for coping. Setting aside just a few minutes each day to write about your experiences can help reduce the mental load of stress and provide a sense of release. Over time, journaling can become a valuable tool for self-reflection and emotional regulation.

Physical Activity for Reducing Stress

Engaging in regular physical activity is a proven way to manage stress and anxiety, as it helps to release endorphins, the body's natural mood enhancers. Exercise also serves as a distraction from worries, providing a mental break from the sources of stress. Whether it's a brisk walk, yoga, or a more intense workout, physical activity can help to clear the mind and reduce the physiological effects of stress, such as muscle tension and increased heart rate. Incorporating movement into your daily routine can make a significant difference in how you manage stress and anxiety, contributing to overall emotional balance and well-being.

Creating a Personal Stress-Management Plan

To effectively manage stress and anxiety, it's important to develop a personalized plan that incorporates a variety of techniques suited to your needs. Start by identifying the specific sources of stress and anxiety in your life, and consider which techniques resonate most with you— whether it's mindful breathing, meditation, journaling, or physical activity. Set realistic goals for incorporating these practices into your daily routine and be consistent in your efforts. Remember that managing stress and anxiety is an ongoing process, and it's okay to adjust your plan as needed. By proactively addressing stress and anxiety, you can build resilience and maintain emotional balance in the face of life's challenges.

The Long-Term Benefits of Stress and Anxiety Management

Consistently practicing techniques for managing stress and anxiety can lead to significant long-term benefits, including improved mental health, better physical health, and enhanced emotional resilience. By reducing the impact of stress and anxiety, you can improve your ability to focus, make decisions, and maintain positive relationships. Over time, these practices can lead to a greater sense of well-being and fulfillment, as you develop the tools needed to navigate life's ups and downs with greater ease. Ultimately, managing stress and anxiety is about creating a sustainable approach to emotional health that supports your overall quality of life.

4.3 Responding vs. Reacting: The Mindful Approach to Emotional Regulation

Understanding the Difference between Responding and Reacting

The concepts of responding and reacting are fundamental to emotional regulation, particularly when practicing mindfulness. Reacting is often an automatic, immediate response to an emotional stimulus, driven by habitual patterns or reflexive behaviors. This reaction typically lacks consideration of the broader context or long-term consequences. In contrast, responding involves a more deliberate and thoughtful approach to managing emotions. It requires pausing to assess the situation, considering various options, and choosing a course of action that aligns with one's values and goals. Mindfulness plays a crucial role in fostering the ability to respond rather than react, by creating the mental space needed to pause and reflect before taking action.

The Role of Mindfulness in Creating Space for Response

Mindfulness helps in creating the crucial pause between stimulus and reaction, which is essential for effective emotional regulation. When we practice mindfulness, we develop greater awareness of our thoughts, emotions, and physical sensations in the present moment. This heightened awareness allows us to notice our initial emotional reactions without immediately acting on them. By recognizing our emotions as they arise, we can take a step back and evaluate our response options more objectively. This pause provides the opportunity to choose a more considered and appropriate response, rather than reacting impulsively based on habitual patterns. Through regular mindfulness practice, this ability to pause and reflect becomes more ingrained, leading to more balanced and thoughtful emotional responses.

The Impact of Automatic Reactions on Emotional Health

Automatic reactions can often lead to negative outcomes, as they are typically driven by unexamined emotional triggers and biases. For example, an immediate defensive reaction to criticism might escalate a conflict, rather than resolving it constructively. These knee-jerk reactions can strain relationships, increase stress, and contribute to overall emotional instability. By contrast, responding with mindfulness allows for a more measured approach, reducing the likelihood of escalating conflicts or making decisions that one might later regret. Over time, habitual reactions can create a pattern of emotional reactivity that undermines long-term emotional health. Practicing mindfulness helps to break this cycle by fostering more deliberate and conscious responses.

Techniques for Cultivating the Mindful Response

Cultivating the mindful response involves several techniques that help bridge the gap between stimulus and action. One effective technique is the use of mindful breathing to create a pause before responding. By taking a few deep, mindful breaths, we can calm our nervous system and bring ourselves back to the present moment. This pause allows us to assess our emotions and choose a response that aligns with our values and intentions. Another technique is to practice mindful observation, which involves observing our emotional responses without judgment. By acknowledging our emotions and their underlying causes, we can respond more thoughtfully rather than reacting out of habit. Additionally, mindfulness-based cognitive techniques, such as reframing negative thoughts and practicing self-compassion, can help us approach emotional situations with greater clarity and empathy.

Applying Mindfulness in Everyday Situations

Applying mindfulness in everyday situations requires practice and consistency. It involves bringing mindful awareness to various aspects of daily life, such as interactions with others, decision-making processes, and responses to stress. For instance, during a heated conversation, mindfulness can help us remain aware of our emotional state and choose a response that fosters constructive dialogue rather than escalating tensions. Similarly, in decision-making scenarios, mindfulness allows us to consider our options more carefully and choose actions that align with our long-term goals. By integrating mindfulness into routine activities, we can enhance our ability to respond thoughtfully and effectively in a wide range of situations.

The Benefits of Mindful Responding to Relationships

Mindful responding significantly benefits interpersonal relationships by fostering more thoughtful and empathetic interactions. When we respond mindfully, we are more likely to consider the perspectives and feelings of others, leading to more compassionate and effective communication. This approach helps to reduce misunderstandings, prevent conflicts, and build stronger connections with others. For example, responding with mindfulness in a disagreement allows us to listen actively and address concerns without reacting defensively. Over time, this mindful approach to communication can enhance trust, cooperation, and overall relationship satisfaction.

Building a Practice of Mindful Emotional Regulation

Developing a practice of mindful emotional regulation involves incorporating mindfulness techniques into daily routines and reflecting on their impact. Start by setting aside time each day for formal mindfulness practices, such as meditation or mindful breathing, and gradually apply these techniques in real-life situations. Reflect on your experiences with mindful responding, noting any changes in your emotional responses and interactions. By consistently practicing mindfulness and building self-awareness, you can strengthen your ability to respond thoughtfully and manage emotions more effectively.

The Long-Term Impact of Mindful Responding

The long-term impact of mindful responding is profound, leading to greater emotional stability, improved relationships, and enhanced overall well-being. As mindfulness becomes a regular part of your emotional regulation practice, you will find that you are better equipped to handle life's challenges with a calm and balanced perspective. Mindful responding fosters resilience, reduces the impact of stress, and promotes a more fulfilling and harmonious life. By continuously practicing and integrating mindfulness into your daily routine, you can achieve a more balanced and intentional approach to emotional regulation, leading to lasting improvements in your emotional health and quality of life.

Chapter 5: Developing Compassion for Yourself and Others

Understanding Compassion and Its Importance

Compassion is the ability to empathize with others' suffering and take action to alleviate it. It involves both a deep understanding of the pain others are experiencing and a desire to support them in their time of need. Compassion extends not only to others but also to oneself, encompassing self-kindness and understanding in moments of struggle. Developing compassion is crucial for building strong relationships, enhancing emotional well-being, and creating a supportive community. It fosters a sense of connection and reduces feelings of isolation, making it a vital aspect of emotional intelligence and overall mental health.

The Role of Self-Compassion

Self-compassion involves treating oneself with the same kindness and understanding that one would offer a friend facing difficulties. It is a critical component of emotional resilience, helping individuals navigate personal challenges with greater ease. Self-compassion allows people to accept their flaws and mistakes without harsh self-criticism, promoting a healthier and more balanced self-view. By practicing self-compassion, individuals can mitigate feelings of guilt, shame, and inadequacy, which often accompany personal setbacks. This compassionate approach supports emotional healing and encourages a more positive and forgiving relationship with oneself.

Cultivating Self-Compassion

Cultivating self-compassion involves several practical strategies. One effective method is to practice self-kindness, which means treating oneself with gentleness and care during difficult times. This can be achieved by speaking to oneself in a supportive and encouraging manner, rather than engaging in self-criticism. Another technique is mindfulness, which involves observing one's thoughts and emotions without judgment. By acknowledging and accepting personal struggles without over-identifying with them, individuals can foster a more compassionate internal dialogue. Additionally, engaging in self-care activities that nurture physical and emotional well-being—such as exercise, relaxation, and hobbies—can further reinforce a compassionate attitude towards oneself.

Extending Compassion to Others

Extending compassion to others involves recognizing and responding to their suffering with empathy and kindness. This practice can significantly enhance interpersonal relationships and build a supportive environment. To extend compassion effectively, it is important to actively listen to others and validate their feelings, demonstrating genuine concern and understanding. Empathizing with others requires putting oneself in their shoes and appreciating their perspectives, which fosters a deeper connection and mutual respect. Acts of kindness, whether through emotional support, practical assistance, or simply being present, contribute to a compassionate approach to others' needs.

Practicing Empathy as a Foundation for Compassion

Empathy is a foundational element of compassion, as it involves understanding and sharing the feelings of others. Developing empathy requires attentive listening and emotional attunement, allowing individuals to connect with others on a deeper level. One way to enhance empathy is by engaging in reflective listening, where you paraphrase and acknowledge the speaker's emotions to show that you are fully present and understand their experience. Another approach is to practice perspective-taking, which involves imagining oneself in another's situation and considering their thoughts and feelings. By cultivating empathy, individuals can more effectively respond to others' needs with genuine compassion.

Overcoming Barriers to Compassion

Several barriers can hinder the development of compassion, both towards oneself and others. Common obstacles include personal biases, emotional exhaustion, and societal norms that prioritize individual success over collective well-being. Overcoming these barriers involves recognizing and addressing the factors that impede compassionate behavior. For example, challenging personal biases requires self-reflection and a willingness to confront prejudiced attitudes. Emotional exhaustion can be managed by setting healthy boundaries and practicing self-care. Additionally, fostering a compassionate mindset often involves countering societal pressures by prioritizing kindness and connection over competition and achievement.

The Benefits of Compassionate Living

Living a compassionate life offers numerous benefits, including improved emotional health, stronger relationships, and a greater sense of fulfillment. Compassionate individuals often experience higher levels of happiness and lower levels of stress, as they are more likely to engage in supportive social interactions and receive reciprocal kindness. Compassion also contributes to a sense of purpose and belonging, as individuals feel more connected to their communities and valued by others. Additionally, practicing compassion can lead to positive ripple effects, inspiring others to adopt similar attitudes and creating a more empathetic and supportive environment.

Integrating Compassion into Daily Life

Integrating compassion into daily life involves consistently applying compassionate practices in everyday interactions and decision-making. This can be achieved by making a conscious effort to act with kindness, whether through small gestures of support or larger acts of service. Regularly reflecting on one's interactions and considering how they align with compassionate values can help maintain a compassionate mindset. Additionally, engaging in activities that promote personal growth and empathy, such as volunteering or participating in community initiatives, can reinforce a commitment to compassionate living.

The Long-Term Impact of Developing Compassion

The long-term impact of developing compassion is profound, leading to lasting improvements in personal well-being and relational dynamics. Over time, cultivating compassion enhances emotional resilience, fosters more meaningful relationships, and contributes to a greater sense of life satisfaction. By consistently practicing self-compassion and extending kindness to others, individuals create a positive feedback loop that strengthens their emotional health and overall quality of life. Compassionate living not only benefits individuals but also contributes to a more empathetic and supportive society, promoting collective well-being and harmony.

5.1 The Importance of Self-Compassion

Defining Self-Compassion

Self-compassion involves treating oneself with the same kindness, concern, and support that one would offer to a close friend in times of difficulty. It is an essential component of emotional well-being and resilience, offering a nurturing response to personal failures and struggles. Unlike self-esteem, which is often based on comparisons and achievements, self-compassion is rooted in unconditional self-acceptance and understanding. It encompasses three core elements: self-kindness, common humanity, and mindfulness. Self-kindness involves being gentle and understanding with oneself during times of suffering. Common humanity refers to recognizing that personal struggles are part of the shared human experience, rather than viewing them as unique or isolating. Mindfulness entails observing one's experiences without over-identification or judgment, allowing for a balanced perspective on personal challenges.

The Impact of Self-Compassion on Emotional Resilience

Self-compassion plays a crucial role in building emotional resilience, which is the ability to bounce back from adversity and cope with stress. When individuals practice self-compassion, they create a supportive internal environment that fosters emotional stability and reduces the impact of negative experiences. This compassionate approach allows for a healthier response to setbacks and failures, as individuals are less likely to engage in harsh self-criticism or self-blame. By treating oneself with kindness and understanding, individuals can maintain a sense of self-worth and motivation, even in the face of challenges. This resilience enables them to approach difficulties with a more adaptive and constructive mindset, leading to better overall mental health and well-being.

Reducing Self-Criticism Through Self-Compassion

Self-criticism is a common response to personal mistakes and shortcomings, often leading to increased stress, anxiety, and feelings of inadequacy. Self-compassion offers a powerful antidote to self-criticism by encouraging a more balanced and supportive internal dialogue. Rather than berating oneself for perceived failures, self-compassion involves acknowledging mistakes with a sense of understanding and forgiveness. This shift in perspective helps to reduce the negative emotional impact of self-criticism and promotes a more positive self-view. By practicing self-compassion, individuals can break the cycle of self-criticism and cultivate a more nurturing and accepting attitude towards themselves.

Enhancing Overall Mental Health Through Self-Compassion

Self-compassion contributes significantly to overall mental health by fostering a positive relationship with oneself and reducing the impact of negative emotions. Research has shown that individuals who practice self-compassion experience lower levels of anxiety, depression, and stress. This is because self-compassion provides a buffer against the adverse effects of challenging experiences and negative self-talk. By promoting a more balanced and accepting view of oneself, self-compassion helps to create a stable emotional foundation, supporting better mental health and well-being. Additionally, self-compassion encourages individuals to engage in self-care and healthy coping strategies, further enhancing their mental health and resilience.

Self-Compassion and Personal Growth

Self-compassion also plays a vital role in personal growth and self-improvement. Rather than viewing personal failures and imperfections as obstacles, self-compassion allows individuals to approach them as opportunities for learning and development. By treating oneself with kindness and understanding during times of struggle, individuals can maintain a sense of motivation and optimism. This compassionate approach encourages a growth mindset, where challenges are seen as valuable experiences that contribute to personal growth. As a result, individuals are more likely to embrace their imperfections and pursue self-improvement with a positive and constructive attitude.

Building Self-Compassion Practices

Building self-compassion involves integrating specific practices into daily life that promote kindness and understanding towards oneself. One effective practice is the use of self-compassionate affirmations, where individuals repeat positive statements that reinforce self-kindness and acceptance. Another practice is engaging in self-care activities that nurture physical and emotional well-being, such as exercise, relaxation, and hobbies. Additionally, mindfulness meditation can support the development of self-compassion by increasing awareness of one's thoughts and emotions, allowing for a more balanced and accepting perspective. Regularly reflecting on personal experiences and challenges with a compassionate mindset can further reinforce these practices and contribute to a more self-compassionate attitude.

The Ripple Effect of Self-Compassion

The benefits of self-compassion extend beyond individual well-being, impacting relationships and interactions with others. When individuals practice self-compassion, they are more likely to extend the same kindness and understanding to others, fostering more empathetic and supportive relationships. This ripple effect can enhance social connections, improve communication, and contribute to a more positive and nurturing environment. By cultivating self-compassion, individuals not only improve their emotional health but also create a more compassionate and supportive community, promoting collective well-being and harmony.

Long-Term Benefits of Self-Compassion

The long-term benefits of self-compassion are profound and far-reaching. By consistently practicing self-compassion, individuals can achieve greater emotional stability, resilience, and overall well-being. This compassionate approach supports a more balanced and positive self-view, reduces the impact of negative emotions, and fosters personal growth. Additionally, self-compassion contributes to stronger relationships and a more supportive community, enhancing social connections and collective well-being. As individuals continue to integrate self-compassion into their daily lives, they experience lasting improvements in their emotional health, personal growth, and overall quality of life.

5.2 Practicing Loving-Kindness Meditation

Understanding Loving-Kindness Meditation

Loving-kindness meditation, also known as "Metta" meditation, is a practice aimed at cultivating an attitude of unconditional love and compassion towards oneself and others. Originating from Buddhist traditions, this meditation focuses on developing feelings of goodwill and kindness through a structured process of guided intentions and affirmations. The core objective of loving-kindness meditation is to enhance emotional resilience and foster a deep sense of connection with others. By repeatedly directing positive and loving thoughts towards oneself and others, practitioners work to overcome negative emotions and cultivate a more compassionate and open-hearted mindset.

The Process of Loving-Kindness Meditation

Loving-kindness meditation typically involves a series of steps that guide practitioners through the process of developing compassion and goodwill. The practice begins with finding a comfortable seated position and focusing on deep, relaxed breathing to center the mind. Practitioners then silently repeat specific phrases or affirmations designed to evoke feelings of love and kindness. These phrases are often directed first towards oneself, such as "May I be happy, may I be healthy, may I be safe." After establishing a foundation of self-love, practitioners gradually extend these sentiments to loved ones, acquaintances, and even individuals with whom they have difficulties. The final stage involves extending loving-kindness to all beings universally, promoting a sense of interconnectedness and compassion.

Benefits of Loving-Kindness Meditation

Loving-kindness meditation offers a range of emotional and psychological benefits. Research indicates that regular practice can lead to increased levels of positive emotions, greater life satisfaction, and improved overall well-being. By focusing on generating and receiving loving-kindness, individuals often experience a reduction in stress, anxiety, and depression. The practice also enhances emotional resilience, enabling individuals to better cope with interpersonal conflicts and challenges. Additionally, loving-kindness meditation fosters empathy and compassion, which can strengthen relationships and improve social interactions. The overall effect is a greater sense of inner peace and a more positive outlook on life.

Cultivating Self-Compassion through Loving-Kindness Meditation

One of the primary benefits of loving-kindness meditation is its ability to cultivate self-compassion. By beginning the practice with affirmations directed towards oneself, individuals reinforce a positive and accepting view of themselves. This process helps to counteract self-criticism and negative self-perceptions, promoting a more nurturing and forgiving internal dialogue. As practitioners continue to extend loving-kindness towards themselves, they develop a greater sense of self-worth and acceptance. This enhanced self-compassion contributes to overall emotional well-being and resilience, enabling individuals to approach personal challenges with greater ease and understanding.

Extending Compassion to Others

Loving-kindness meditation also plays a crucial role in extending compassion to others. As practitioners direct loving thoughts towards friends, family, and even individuals they may have conflicts with, they develop a deeper understanding and empathy toward others' experiences and emotions. This process helps to dissolve feelings of anger, resentment, and judgment, fostering more harmonious and supportive relationships. By actively practicing loving-kindness towards others, individuals contribute to a more compassionate and connected community, enhancing social cohesion and mutual support.

Overcoming Challenges in Loving-Kindness Meditation

While loving-kindness meditation offers numerous benefits, practitioners may encounter challenges during the practice. Common obstacles include difficulty maintaining focus, resistance to extending kindness to certain individuals, or feelings of discomfort with self-affirmations. To address these challenges, it is important to approach the practice with patience and persistence. Practitioners can start with shorter sessions and gradually increase the duration as they become more comfortable. It may also be helpful to explore different phrases or affirmations that resonate personally. Additionally, acknowledging and accepting any difficulties or discomfort that arise during the practice can contribute to a more compassionate and understanding approach.

Incorporating Loving-Kindness Meditation into Daily Life

Integrating loving-kindness meditation into daily life involves incorporating its principles and practices into everyday interactions and experiences. This can be achieved by setting aside time each day for formal meditation sessions, as well as applying the principles of loving-kindness in real-life situations. For example, practitioners can consciously offer kind and supportive words to others, engage in acts of service, and practice active listening. By maintaining a consistent practice and applying the principles of loving-kindness in daily interactions, individuals can reinforce their compassionate mindset and enhance their overall emotional well-being.

Long-Term Impact of Loving-Kindness Meditation

The long-term impact of loving-kindness meditation is profound, leading to lasting improvements in emotional health, relationships, and overall quality of life. Regular practice fosters a deep sense of compassion and empathy, contributing to a more positive and supportive outlook on life. Over time, individuals who practice loving-kindness meditation often experience greater emotional resilience, improved interpersonal relationships, and a more fulfilling sense of connection with others. By integrating loving-kindness into daily life, individuals create a ripple effect of compassion and positivity that enhances both personal well-being and collective harmony.

5.3 Building Empathy and Compassion toward Others

Understanding Empathy and Its Role in Compassion

Empathy involves the ability to understand and share the feelings of others, creating a bridge between individual experiences and emotional connections. It is a foundational element of compassion, as it allows individuals to relate to others' suffering and respond with kindness and support. Empathy goes beyond mere sympathy; it requires actively engaging with and feeling the emotions of others, which fosters a deeper connection and understanding. By cultivating empathy, individuals are better equipped to offer genuine compassion and contribute to more supportive and harmonious relationships.

Practicing Active Listening

Active listening is a key technique for building empathy and compassion. It involves fully focusing on and engaging with the speaker, without interrupting or formulating responses while they are talking. Active listening requires paying attention to verbal and non-verbal cues, such as tone of voice, facial expressions, and body language. By reflecting back what the speaker has said and acknowledging their feelings, listeners demonstrate that they value and understand their perspective. This approach not only enhances empathy but also fosters trust and connection, allowing for more meaningful and compassionate interactions.

Engaging in Perspective-Taking

Perspective-taking is another important strategy for building empathy and compassion. It involves imagining oneself in another person's situation and considering their thoughts, feelings, and experiences. This practice helps individuals develop a deeper understanding of others' emotions and viewpoints, which can lead to more compassionate responses. Perspective-taking can be practiced through various exercises, such as discussing hypothetical scenarios, reading diverse literature, or engaging in role-playing activities. By expanding one's perspective, individuals become more attuned to the complexities of others' experiences and are better equipped to offer support and understanding.

Cultivating Emotional Awareness

Cultivating emotional awareness is essential for developing empathy and compassion. This involves recognizing and acknowledging one's own emotions and understanding how they influence interactions with others. Emotional awareness helps individuals become more attuned to the emotional states of those around them, allowing for more empathetic responses. Techniques for enhancing emotional awareness include mindfulness practices, journaling, and self-reflection. By developing a deeper awareness of one's own emotional landscape, individuals can more effectively connect with and support others, leading to more compassionate interactions.

Responding with Compassionate Action

Responding with compassionate action involves translating empathy into concrete behaviors that support and assist others. Compassionate actions can include offering emotional support, providing practical help, or simply being present for someone in need. It is important to approach compassionate action with sensitivity and respect, ensuring that the support offered aligns with the recipient's needs and preferences. By actively engaging in compassionate behaviors, individuals demonstrate their commitment to understanding and addressing the challenges faced by others, reinforcing the principles of empathy and kindness.

Building Empathy through Shared Experiences

Shared experiences can significantly enhance empathy and compassion. Engaging in activities or discussions that highlight commonalities and shared challenges fosters a sense of connection and mutual understanding. For example, participating in community service projects or support groups can provide opportunities to connect with others who are facing similar struggles. These shared experiences help individuals relate to each other's emotions and perspectives, deepening their empathy and compassion. Additionally, sharing personal stories and experiences with others can create a sense of solidarity and reinforce the understanding of common human experiences.

Overcoming Barriers to Empathy

Overcoming barriers to empathy involves addressing factors that impede the ability to connect with and understand others. Common barriers include personal biases, judgment, and emotional distance. To overcome these challenges, it is important to practice self-awareness and reflect on any biases or assumptions that may affect empathetic interactions. Engaging in open-minded discussions and actively seeking diverse perspectives can help mitigate these barriers. Additionally, addressing emotional distance by practicing self-compassion and managing personal stress can create a more receptive mindset for empathizing with others.

Integrating Empathy and Compassion into Daily Life

Integrating empathy and compassion into daily life involves consistently applying these principles in various interactions and situations. This can be achieved by making a conscious effort to listen actively, offer support, and compassionately engage with others. Practicing empathy and compassion in everyday interactions, such as conversations with colleagues, friends, and family members, helps reinforce these values and build stronger relationships. By incorporating empathy and compassion into daily routines and interactions, individuals create a positive ripple effect that enhances personal well-being and fosters a more supportive and empathetic community.

The Long-Term Impact of Empathy and Compassion

The long-term impact of building empathy and compassion is profound, leading to enhanced emotional well-being, improved relationships, and a more connected community. Individuals who cultivate empathy and compassion often experience greater satisfaction in their personal and professional relationships, as they are better able to understand and support others. Additionally, the practice of empathy and compassion contributes to a more positive and harmonious social environment, fostering a sense of community and mutual support. Over time, these values create lasting improvements in both individual and collective well-being, promoting a more compassionate and interconnected world.

Chapter 6: Enhancing Social Skills through Emotional Intelligence

The Link Between Emotional Intelligence and Social Skills

Emotional intelligence plays a critical role in developing and enhancing social skills. It involves the ability to recognize, understand, and manage one's own emotions, as well as the emotions of others. Social skills are the tools we use to interact and communicate effectively with others, and they are heavily influenced by our emotional intelligence. When individuals are attuned to their emotions and those of others, they can navigate social situations with greater ease, foster positive relationships, and handle conflicts more effectively. Emotional intelligence forms the foundation of essential social skills such as communication, empathy, conflict resolution, and collaboration.

Effective Communication: The Heart of Social Skills

Effective communication is at the core of all social interactions and is a key component of emotional intelligence. It involves both verbal and non-verbal communication, such as body language, tone of voice, and facial expressions. Emotional intelligence enhances communication by enabling individuals to convey their thoughts and feelings clearly and to interpret the emotions and intentions behind others' words and actions. This understanding helps to avoid misunderstandings, build trust, and foster meaningful connections. Additionally, emotionally intelligent communication involves active listening, which ensures that all parties feel heard and respected, further strengthening social bonds.

Building Stronger Relationships through Emotional Intelligence

Emotional intelligence is essential for building and maintaining strong relationships, whether personal or professional. By understanding and managing their own emotions, individuals can approach relationships with a greater sense of self-awareness and control, reducing the likelihood of conflict and miscommunication. Emotional intelligence also fosters empathy, allowing individuals to see things from others' perspectives and respond with compassion and understanding. This empathy helps to create deeper, more meaningful connections and promotes mutual respect and trust. Additionally, emotionally intelligent individuals are better equipped to navigate the complexities of relationships, addressing challenges with patience and sensitivity.

Conflict Resolution and Emotional Intelligence

Conflict is an inevitable part of any social interaction, but emotional intelligence can greatly enhance one's ability to resolve conflicts effectively. Emotionally intelligent individuals are better at recognizing the emotions driving the conflict, both in themselves and others, which allows them to approach the situation with greater empathy and understanding. They can stay calm and composed, avoiding emotional outbursts or defensive reactions that can escalate the conflict. Instead, they focus on finding a solution that addresses the underlying emotional needs of all parties involved. This approach not only resolves the immediate conflict but also strengthens relationships and builds trust over time.

Collaboration and Teamwork Enhanced by Emotional Intelligence

Collaboration and teamwork are essential social skills in both personal and professional settings, and emotional intelligence significantly enhances these skills. In a team environment, emotional intelligence helps individuals understand and appreciate the diverse perspectives and emotions of their team members. This understanding fosters a more inclusive and supportive environment where everyone feels valued and respected. Emotionally intelligent individuals are also better at managing their emotions in collaborative settings, remaining calm under pressure, and providing constructive feedback without offending. This emotional regulation promotes a positive team dynamic, encourages open communication, and leads to more effective collaboration and successful outcomes.

The Role of Emotional Intelligence in Leadership

Leadership is a social skill that is greatly enhanced by emotional intelligence. Leaders with high emotional intelligence are better equipped to inspire and motivate others, build strong teams, and navigate the complexities of organizational dynamics. They can recognize and respond to the emotional needs of their team members, providing support and guidance when needed. Emotionally intelligent leaders are also more adept at handling stress and making decisions under pressure, which helps them maintain stability and focus within their teams. By fostering a culture of empathy, understanding, and collaboration, emotionally intelligent leaders can create a positive and productive work environment.

Developing Emotional Intelligence for Social Skill Enhancement

Enhancing social skills through emotional intelligence requires ongoing self-reflection and practice. Individuals can develop their emotional intelligence by regularly engaging in mindfulness practices, which help to increase self-awareness and emotional regulation. Additionally, seeking feedback from others and being open to constructive criticism can provide valuable insights into how one's emotions and behaviors impact social interactions. Developing empathy by actively listening to and understanding others' perspectives is also crucial for improving social skills. By continuously working on these aspects of emotional intelligence, individuals can enhance their ability to navigate social situations effectively, build stronger relationships, and achieve greater personal and professional success.

The Long-Term Impact of Enhanced Social Skills

The long-term impact of enhancing social skills through emotional intelligence is significant. Individuals who invest in developing their emotional intelligence and social skills are likely to experience more fulfilling and successful relationships in both their personal and professional lives. They can communicate more effectively, resolve conflicts with ease, and collaborate more successfully with others. These skills also contribute to greater overall emotional well-being, as emotionally intelligent individuals are better equipped to handle the challenges and complexities of social interactions. Over time, the continuous improvement of social skills through emotional intelligence leads to stronger connections, increased satisfaction, and a more harmonious and productive social life.

6.1 Mindful Communication and Active Listening

The Essence of Mindful Communication

Mindful communication is the practice of being fully present and engaged during interactions with others. It involves speaking with intention, clarity, and awareness of both one's own emotions and the emotions of others. Unlike ordinary communication, where distractions or emotional reactions may interfere, mindful communication emphasizes a deliberate and thoughtful approach. This requires being aware of the impact of words, tone, and body language on the listener. Practicing mindful communication means pausing before responding, ensuring that what is said is both necessary and constructive. This approach helps prevent misunderstandings and fosters a more respectful and effective exchange of ideas.

The Role of Emotional Intelligence in Mindful Communication

Emotional intelligence is integral to mindful communication. By understanding and managing one's own emotions, individuals can communicate more effectively and avoid emotional reactions that may derail a conversation. For example, someone with high emotional intelligence is likely to recognize when they are becoming frustrated and can take a moment to calm down before responding, thus maintaining a constructive dialogue. Similarly, being attuned to the emotions of others allows for more empathetic and considerate communication. This sensitivity to emotional cues helps in adjusting the message to better suit the listener's emotional state, thereby enhancing the effectiveness of communication.

Active Listening: A Core Component of Mindful Communication

Active listening is a crucial aspect of mindful communication and involves fully concentrating, understanding, and responding to what is being said. Unlike passive listening, where the listener might be distracted or simply waiting for their turn to speak, active listening requires full attention to the speaker. This includes not only hearing the words but also understanding the underlying emotions and intentions. Active listening involves techniques such as nodding in agreement, maintaining eye contact, and summarizing what the speaker has said to confirm understanding. By demonstrating that the listener is fully engaged, active listening builds trust and strengthens relationships.

Techniques for Practicing Active Listening

To practice active listening, it is essential to focus on the speaker without distractions. This means putting away phones, avoiding interrupting, and paying close attention to both verbal and non-verbal cues. Reflecting on what the speaker has said by paraphrasing or summarizing their points helps to ensure understanding and shows that their message has been heard. Asking open-ended questions can also encourage the speaker to elaborate and clarify their thoughts, further deepening the conversation. Another technique is to observe the speaker's body language and tone of voice, as these can provide important insights into their emotional state, allowing for a more empathetic response.

The Benefits of Combining Mindful Communication and Active Listening

Combining mindful communication with active listening creates a powerful approach to social interactions. This combination ensures that conversations are both respectful and productive, with each party feeling heard and valued. Mindful communication reduces the likelihood of misunderstandings and conflicts by fostering clarity and intentionality in speech. Meanwhile, active listening ensures that the speaker's message is fully understood, reducing the risk of miscommunication. Together, these practices enhance the overall quality of interactions, leading to stronger relationships, greater mutual respect, and more effective collaboration in both personal and professional settings.

Challenges in Practicing Mindful Communication and Active Listening

Despite its benefits, practicing mindful communication and active listening can be challenging, particularly in high-stress or emotionally charged situations. It requires a conscious effort to remain present and engaged, which can be difficult when distractions are present or when emotions run high. Additionally, it can be challenging to resist the urge to interrupt or to mentally prepare a response while the other person is speaking. Overcoming these challenges requires practice and a commitment to improving one's emotional intelligence. By developing self-awareness and learning to manage distractions, individuals can enhance their ability to communicate mindfully and listen actively.

Applying Mindful Communication in Various Contexts

Mindful communication and active listening are applicable in various contexts, from personal relationships to professional environments. In the workplace, these skills can improve team dynamics, enhance leadership effectiveness, and foster a more collaborative atmosphere. In personal relationships, mindful communication can lead to deeper connections and more meaningful interactions. Practicing these skills in everyday conversations, such as during meetings, social gatherings, or family discussions, can significantly improve the quality of interactions. Over time, these practices become more natural, leading to more fulfilling and harmonious relationships across all areas of life.

The Long-Term Impact of Mindful Communication

The long-term impact of practicing mindful communication and active listening is profound. Individuals who consistently apply these skills are likely to experience stronger, more positive relationships, reduced conflicts, and increased emotional well-being. As these practices become habitual, they contribute to a more compassionate and understanding approach to social interactions, benefiting not only the individual but also those around them. The ability to communicate mindfully and listen actively is a valuable skill that enhances both personal and professional success, leading to a more connected and empathetic society.

6.2 Navigating Interpersonal Relationships with Emotional Intelligence

The Role of Emotional Intelligence in Interpersonal Relationships

Emotional intelligence (EI) plays a crucial role in navigating interpersonal relationships, as it provides individuals with the ability to understand and manage both their own emotions and those of others. In any relationship, whether personal or professional, emotions are at the core of interactions. Emotional intelligence enables individuals to recognize emotional cues, respond appropriately, and maintain healthy, balanced relationships. By fostering empathy, self-awareness, and emotional regulation, EI helps to create a foundation of trust and mutual respect, which are essential for sustaining meaningful and productive relationships.

Building Trust through Emotional Awareness

Trust is the cornerstone of any strong relationship, and emotional intelligence is key to building and maintaining that trust. Emotional awareness allows individuals to be honest and transparent about their feelings, which fosters open communication and reduces the likelihood of misunderstandings. When individuals are attuned to their own emotions, they are better equipped to express their needs and concerns without being overwhelmed by negative feelings. Additionally, being aware of the emotions of others helps to create a supportive environment where both parties feel understood and valued. This mutual emotional understanding strengthens the bond of trust and encourages deeper connections.

Effective Conflict Resolution Using Emotional Intelligence

Conflicts are inevitable in any relationship, but emotional intelligence can greatly enhance one's ability to resolve them effectively. EI enables individuals to approach conflicts with a calm and composed demeanor, allowing them to focus on finding a solution rather than becoming defensive or reactive. By recognizing the emotional triggers that lead to conflict, emotionally intelligent individuals can address the root causes rather than just the symptoms. They are also more likely to listen actively to the other party's perspective, demonstrating empathy and understanding. This approach not only resolves the immediate conflict but also strengthens the relationship by fostering greater respect and communication.

Enhancing Empathy and Understanding in Relationships

Empathy, a core component of emotional intelligence, is vital for navigating interpersonal relationships. It involves the ability to put oneself in another's shoes, and understand their emotions and perspectives. This deep level of understanding helps to build stronger, more compassionate relationships. When individuals practice empathy, they are more likely to respond to others with kindness and consideration, which can prevent misunderstandings and reduce tension. Empathy also plays a crucial role in fostering emotional connections, as it allows individuals to relate to one another on a deeper level. By enhancing empathy, emotional intelligence contributes to more harmonious and fulfilling relationships.

The Importance of Emotional Regulation in Maintaining Balance

Emotional regulation is another critical aspect of emotional intelligence that is essential for maintaining balance in relationships. It involves the ability to manage and control one's emotions, particularly in challenging situations. Without emotional regulation, individuals may react impulsively, leading to unnecessary conflicts or strained relationships. By practicing emotional regulation, individuals can respond to situations thoughtfully and with greater emotional control. This not only prevents the escalation of negative emotions but also ensures that interactions remain respectful and constructive. Maintaining emotional balance through regulation helps to preserve the stability of relationships, even during times of stress or disagreement.

Strengthening Communication through Emotional Intelligence

Effective communication is the backbone of any successful relationship, and emotional intelligence enhances this by improving both verbal and non-verbal communication skills. When individuals are emotionally intelligent, they can express their thoughts and feelings clearly and respectfully, without letting emotions cloud their message. They are also better at reading the emotional cues of others, allowing them to respond appropriately and avoid misunderstandings. This leads to more meaningful and productive conversations, where both parties feel heard and valued. Strengthening communication through emotional intelligence helps to build stronger, more connected relationships, as it fosters an environment of mutual respect and understanding.

Navigating Professional Relationships with Emotional Intelligence

In professional settings, emotional intelligence is equally important for navigating relationships with colleagues, clients, and superiors. It allows individuals to manage workplace dynamics effectively, handle conflicts with diplomacy, and collaborate more successfully with others. Emotionally intelligent professionals are often seen as approachable and empathetic, which can enhance their leadership qualities and build stronger teams. By recognizing the emotions of others, they can provide support when needed and create a positive work environment. This not only improves individual relationships but also contributes to overall organizational success, as emotionally intelligent interactions lead to better teamwork and higher morale.

The Long-Term Impact of Emotional Intelligence on Relationships

The long-term impact of emotional intelligence on interpersonal relationships is profound. By continuously developing and applying emotional intelligence, individuals can build stronger, more resilient relationships that stand the test of time. The ability to navigate emotions, communicate effectively, and resolve conflicts constructively leads to deeper connections and greater mutual respect. Over time, these emotionally intelligent practices contribute to more fulfilling personal lives and more successful professional careers. The ongoing cultivation of emotional intelligence ensures that relationships remain healthy, balanced, and enriching, ultimately leading to a more harmonious and connected life.

6.3 The Role of Empathy in Social Interactions

Understanding Empathy and Its Importance

Empathy is the ability to understand and share the feelings of another person. It is a fundamental component of emotional intelligence and plays a crucial role in social interactions. Unlike sympathy, which involves feeling pity or sorrow for someone else's misfortune, empathy requires putting oneself in another's shoes and experiencing their emotions as if they were one's own. This deep level of emotional connection fosters stronger, more authentic relationships, as it allows individuals to respond to others with genuine care and consideration. Empathy is essential for building trust, enhancing communication, and creating a supportive social environment.

Empathy as a Bridge in Communication

In social interactions, empathy acts as a bridge between people, enabling more effective communication. When individuals approach conversations with empathy, they are better able to listen without judgment, understand the underlying emotions behind words, and respond in a way that validates the other person's feelings. This empathetic approach to communication reduces the likelihood of misunderstandings and conflicts, as it encourages openness and mutual respect. By acknowledging and responding to the emotional needs of others, empathy facilitates more meaningful and productive exchanges, whether in personal relationships or professional settings.

The Role of Empathy in Conflict Resolution

Empathy is particularly valuable in conflict resolution, where understanding the emotions and perspectives of others can lead to more peaceful and constructive outcomes. When conflicts arise, emotions often run high, and it can be challenging to see the situation from another's viewpoint. However, by practicing empathy, individuals can step back from their emotional responses and consider the feelings and motivations of others involved. This broader perspective allows for more compassionate and fair solutions, as it encourages all parties to consider the impact of their actions on others. Empathy thus transforms conflict from a confrontational experience into an opportunity for growth and understanding.

Empathy's Impact on Social Bonding

Empathy plays a vital role in social bonding, as it fosters deep connections between individuals. By empathizing with others, people create emotional bonds that go beyond superficial interactions. These bonds are based on mutual understanding, shared experiences, and a genuine concern for each other's well-being. In friendships, empathy strengthens the sense of closeness and trust, making relationships more resilient in the face of challenges. In romantic relationships, empathy deepens emotional intimacy, allowing partners to connect on a profound emotional level. In professional environments, empathy builds camaraderie and teamwork, as colleagues feel more supported and understood.

The Role of Empathy in Leadership

In leadership, empathy is a powerful tool for fostering a positive and inclusive environment. Leaders who practice empathy are better equipped to understand the needs and concerns of their team members, which enables them to provide the right support and guidance. Empathetic leaders can identify when someone is struggling and offer help before issues escalate. This not only boosts morale but also increases productivity and job satisfaction. Additionally, empathy in leadership encourages open communication and trust, as team members feel that their leader genuinely cares about their well-being. This creates a culture of collaboration and mutual respect, leading to a more effective and harmonious workplace.

Empathy and Cultural Sensitivity

Empathy also plays a crucial role in fostering cultural sensitivity and understanding in diverse social interactions. In today's globalized world, people frequently interact with others from different cultural backgrounds. Empathy allows individuals to appreciate these differences and approach interactions with an open mind. By understanding and respecting cultural norms, values, and emotions, empathy helps to break down barriers and build stronger, more inclusive relationships. This cultural sensitivity is essential for navigating social interactions in multicultural settings, whether in international business, community engagement, or cross-cultural friendships.

Challenges in Practicing Empathy

While empathy is a powerful tool for enhancing social interactions, it can also present challenges. Empathizing with others requires emotional energy and can be draining, especially when dealing with negative or intense emotions. Additionally, in situations where there are conflicting needs or perspectives, maintaining empathy for all parties can be difficult. It is also possible to become overwhelmed by the emotions of others, leading to emotional burnout. To address these challenges, it is important to balance empathy with self-care, ensuring that one's emotional well-being is maintained while supporting others. Developing emotional boundaries can also help to manage the intensity of empathetic interactions.

Cultivating Empathy in Daily Life

Cultivating empathy in daily life requires conscious effort and practice. One effective way to develop empathy is by actively listening to others and trying to understand their perspectives without judgment. Engaging in open and honest conversations, where both parties feel safe to express their emotions, can also enhance empathy. Reflecting on one's own experiences and emotions can help to build a deeper understanding of others' feelings. Additionally, mindfulness practices can increase self-awareness and empathy by encouraging individuals to be present and attuned to the emotions of those around them. Over time, these practices can lead to a more empathetic approach to all social interactions.

The Long-Term Impact of Empathy on Social Interactions

The long-term impact of empathy on social interactions is profound, as it leads to stronger, more meaningful relationships and a greater sense of community. Empathy fosters an environment of understanding, compassion, and mutual respect, which enhances the quality of social connections. Over time, these empathetic interactions contribute to a more supportive and inclusive society, where individuals feel valued and understood. By continuously practicing and cultivating empathy, individuals can create lasting positive change in their relationships and social environments, leading to a more connected and compassionate world.

Chapter 7: Overcoming Emotional Challenges with Mindfulness

Understanding Emotional Challenges

Emotional challenges are an inevitable part of life, manifesting in various forms such as stress, anxiety, anger, and sadness. These challenges can arise from personal experiences, relationships, work, or external pressures, and they often disrupt emotional balance, leading to feelings of overwhelm or helplessness. Understanding the nature of these challenges is the first step toward overcoming them. Emotional challenges are not just psychological experiences; they also have physical and behavioral manifestations, such as tension, fatigue, or withdrawal from social activities. Recognizing the signs and triggers of emotional challenges is essential for addressing them effectively and preventing them from escalating.

The Role of Mindfulness in Addressing Emotional Challenges

Mindfulness plays a pivotal role in addressing emotional challenges by promoting a non-judgmental awareness of the present moment. Instead of reacting impulsively to negative emotions, mindfulness encourages individuals to observe their feelings with curiosity and acceptance. This mindful approach allows for a deeper understanding of the emotions at play, reducing their intensity and creating space for a more measured response. By focusing on the present moment, mindfulness helps to break the cycle of rumination and worry, which often exacerbates emotional distress. Through consistent mindfulness practice, individuals can develop greater emotional resilience, enabling them to navigate challenges with greater ease and stability.

Mindfulness Techniques for Managing Stress

Stress is one of the most common emotional challenges, often triggered by external pressures such as work, relationships, or life changes. Mindfulness offers effective techniques for managing stress by bringing attention to the body and breathing, which can calm the nervous system and reduce the physiological impact of stress. Techniques such as mindful breathing, body scanning, and progressive muscle relaxation can help to release tension and promote a sense of calm. Additionally, mindfulness meditation can shift focus away from stressors, allowing individuals to gain perspective and respond more thoughtfully rather than reacting impulsively. Over time, these practices can significantly reduce stress levels and enhance overall well-being.

Addressing Anxiety with Mindfulness

Anxiety is another prevalent emotional challenge, characterized by excessive worry, fear, or apprehension about future events. Mindfulness helps to address anxiety by grounding individuals in the present moment, where anxiety often has less power. Techniques such as mindful observation, where one focuses on immediate sensory experiences, can divert attention away from anxious thoughts and reduce their impact. Mindfulness also teaches acceptance, encouraging individuals to acknowledge anxious feelings without judgment or resistance, which can diminish their hold. By regularly practicing mindfulness, individuals can develop a greater tolerance for uncertainty and a calmer approach to potential challenges, reducing the frequency and intensity of anxiety.

Using Mindfulness to Navigate Anger

Anger is a powerful emotion that can be difficult to manage, often leading to impulsive actions and strained relationships. Mindfulness provides tools for navigating anger by encouraging individuals to pause and observe their emotional state before reacting. This pause creates a buffer between the emotion and the response, allowing for more thoughtful and controlled actions. Mindful practices such as deep breathing, counting to ten, or engaging in a quick meditation can help to diffuse the intensity of anger. Over time, mindfulness can also reveal the underlying causes of anger, such as unmet needs or unresolved issues, enabling individuals to address these root causes constructively rather than lashing out.

Dealing with Sadness through Mindfulness

Sadness is a natural emotional response to loss, disappointment, or other challenging experiences. While it is a normal part of life, prolonged sadness can lead to feelings of hopelessness or depression. Mindfulness offers a way to approach sadness with compassion and acceptance, allowing individuals to process their emotions without being overwhelmed by them. By observing sadness mindfully, individuals can identify the thoughts and beliefs that contribute to their emotional state, and gently challenge any unhelpful patterns. Mindfulness also encourages self-care practices, such as connecting with loved ones, engaging in enjoyable activities, or practicing self-compassion, which can alleviate sadness and promote healing.

Building Emotional Resilience with Mindfulness

Emotional resilience is the ability to bounce back from emotional challenges and maintain a sense of well-being despite adversity. Mindfulness contributes to emotional resilience by fostering a balanced and flexible approach to emotions. Through mindfulness, individuals learn to accept their emotions without being controlled by them, which reduces the impact of negative experiences and enhances the ability to recover from setbacks. Mindfulness also cultivates a positive outlook by encouraging gratitude and presence, which can shift focus away from negative emotions and towards more constructive thoughts and actions. With regular practice, mindfulness strengthens emotional resilience, enabling individuals to face life's challenges with greater confidence and inner strength.

The Long-Term Impact of Mindfulness on Emotional Challenges

The long-term impact of mindfulness on emotional challenges is profound. As individuals continue to practice mindfulness, they develop a deeper understanding of their emotional landscape and a greater ability to manage their emotions effectively. This leads to a more stable and balanced emotional state, where challenges are met with calmness and clarity rather than reactivity or distress. Over time, mindfulness transforms the way individuals relate to their emotions, fostering a sense of peace and equanimity that persists even in the face of adversity. By integrating mindfulness into daily life, individuals can overcome emotional challenges with greater ease and create a more fulfilling and harmonious life experience.

7.1 Dealing with Negative Emotions Mindfully

Understanding Negative Emotions

Negative emotions such as anger, fear, sadness, and frustration are a natural part of the human experience. These emotions often arise in response to difficult situations, perceived threats, or unmet needs. While negative emotions are sometimes viewed as undesirable, they serve important functions, such as signaling when something is wrong or motivating us to make necessary changes in our lives. However, when these emotions become overwhelming or persistent, they can disrupt our mental and physical well-being. Mindfulness offers a way to approach negative emotions with curiosity and acceptance, rather than avoiding or suppressing them.

Acknowledging and Accepting Emotions

One of the key principles of mindfulness is the practice of acknowledging and accepting emotions as they arise, without judgment. This means recognizing the presence of negative emotions without labeling them as "bad" or trying to push them away. Acceptance does not mean resigning to these emotions, but rather allowing them to exist in the present moment without resistance. By accepting emotions, individuals can prevent them from becoming more intense or prolonged.

This mindful approach creates space for understanding the root causes of negative emotions and addressing them more effectively.

Observing Emotions without Attachment

Mindfulness encourages observing negative emotions as temporary experiences that do not define us. Instead of identifying with the emotion ("I am angry"), mindfulness promotes a perspective that separates the self from the emotion ("I am experiencing anger"). This detachment helps to reduce the power that negative emotions hold over our thoughts and behaviors. By observing emotions without attachment, individuals can gain clarity on the triggers and patterns associated with these emotions, leading to more conscious and deliberate responses. This practice also helps in recognizing that emotions, like all experiences, are impermanent and will eventually pass.

Breathing Techniques for Emotional Regulation

Mindful breathing is a powerful tool for managing negative emotions. When emotions such as anger or anxiety arise, the body's fight-or-flight response is often triggered, leading to physical symptoms like rapid heartbeat, shallow breathing, and muscle tension. Mindful breathing helps to counteract this response by activating the parasympathetic nervous system, which promotes relaxation and calmness. Techniques such as deep belly breathing, where the breath is drawn deep into the abdomen, can slow the heart rate and reduce tension. Focusing on the breath also serves as an anchor, bringing attention back to the present moment and away from ruminative thoughts.

Reframing Negative Thoughts

Negative emotions are often accompanied by negative thoughts, which can perpetuate and intensify emotional distress. Mindfulness encourages the practice of reframing these thoughts, which involves identifying and challenging unhelpful cognitive patterns. For example, thoughts such as "I will never succeed" can be reinterpreted as "I am facing challenges, but I can overcome them." This shift in perspective can reduce the intensity of negative emotions and promote a more balanced and constructive mindset. Mindful reframing is not about forcing positive thinking but rather about cultivating a more realistic and compassionate view of oneself and the situation.

Using Mindfulness to Process Emotions

Processing emotions mindfully involves giving oneself the time and space to fully experience and explore emotions without rushing to resolve them. This can be done through practices such as mindful journaling, where individuals write about their emotions in a non-judgmental way, or through mindful movements, such as yoga or walking, which can help to release emotional tension stored in the body. By processing emotions mindfully, individuals can gain deeper insights into their emotional experiences and develop a greater sense of emotional clarity and acceptance. This process can lead to emotional healing and a stronger sense of inner peace.

The Role of Compassion in Dealing with Negative Emotions

Compassion, both for oneself and others, is a crucial component of dealing with negative emotions mindfully. When negative emotions arise, it is common to be self-critical or to blame others, which can exacerbate emotional distress. Mindfulness teaches the importance of responding to negative emotions with kindness and understanding. This involves recognizing that everyone experiences difficult emotions and that it is okay to feel them without judgment. Self-compassion practices, such as offering oneself comforting words or engaging in nurturing activities, can help to soothe negative emotions and promote emotional resilience.

Long-Term Benefits of Mindfully Managing Negative Emotions

The long-term benefits of managing negative emotions mindfully are significant. Over time, mindfulness practices can lead to a more balanced and resilient emotional state, where negative emotions are less likely to overwhelm or dictate one's actions. Individuals who consistently practice mindfulness tend to develop greater emotional intelligence, allowing them to navigate challenges with more ease and composure. This not only enhances personal well-being but also improves relationships and overall life satisfaction. By dealing with negative emotions mindfully, individuals can cultivate a deeper sense of inner peace and emotional stability, even in the face of life's inevitable challenges.

7.2 Techniques for Coping with Emotional Triggers

Understanding Emotional Triggers

Emotional triggers are specific situations, people, or events that evoke intense emotional responses, often rooted in past experiences or unresolved issues. These triggers can lead to feelings of anger, fear, sadness, or frustration and may cause individuals to react impulsively or disproportionately to the situation at hand. Understanding what triggers these emotions is crucial for managing them effectively. Triggers vary widely from person to person, and they often reveal underlying emotional wounds or beliefs that have not been fully processed. By identifying these triggers, individuals can begin to understand their emotional landscape and take steps to cope with them more mindfully.

Mindful Awareness of Triggers

The first step in coping with emotional triggers is cultivating mindful awareness of when and how they occur. This involves paying close attention to the physical sensations, thoughts, and emotions that arise in response to a triggering event. Mindfulness encourages observing these reactions without judgment or immediate action, allowing individuals to create a mental space between the trigger and their response. This space is crucial because it enables a more deliberate and thoughtful reaction rather than a reflexive one. Over time, practicing mindful awareness can help reduce the intensity of emotional reactions to triggers and increase emotional resilience.

Grounding Techniques for Immediate Relief

When an emotional trigger is activated, grounding techniques can provide immediate relief by bringing attention back to the present moment. Grounding involves focusing on something tangible and external to distract from the overwhelming emotions. Techniques such as feeling the texture of an object, listening to ambient sounds, or concentrating on the sensation of feet on the ground can help interrupt the cycle of emotional escalation. Another effective grounding technique is the "5-4-3-2-1" method, which involves identifying five things you can see, four things you can touch, three things you can hear, two things you can smell, and one thing you can taste. These practices can help calm the mind and body, making it easier to manage the triggered emotions.

Breathing Techniques for Emotional Regulation

Breathing is a powerful tool for managing emotional triggers because it directly influences the body's stress response. When emotions are triggered, the body often enters a fight-or-flight mode, characterized by rapid breathing, increased heart rate, and muscle tension. Mindful breathing techniques can counteract this response by activating the parasympathetic nervous system, which promotes relaxation. Techniques such as deep belly breathing, where one inhales deeply through the nose, allowing the diaphragm to expand, and then exhales slowly through the mouth, can help calm the nervous system. Another useful technique is box breathing, which involves inhaling for four counts, holding the breath for four counts, exhaling for four counts, and holding again for four counts. These techniques can be practiced anytime a trigger is recognized, helping to maintain emotional equilibrium.

Cognitive Reframing to Challenge Triggering Thoughts

Cognitive reframing involves changing the way one interprets a triggering situation in order to alter its emotional impact. This technique is rooted in the understanding that our thoughts influence our emotions, and by changing our thoughts, we can change our emotional responses. When faced with a trigger, mindfulness encourages stepping back and questioning the initial thoughts that arise. Are these thoughts based on facts, or are they distorted by past experiences or fears? By reframing the situation in a more balanced and compassionate way, individuals can reduce the emotional charge of the trigger. For example, instead of thinking, "This always happens to me," one might reframe the thought to, "This is a challenging situation, but I have the tools to cope with it."

Creating a Safe Space for Emotional Processing

Creating a safe space, either physically or mentally, can be an effective way to cope with emotional triggers. This might involve finding a quiet place to sit and reflect, engaging in a calming activity such as drawing or journaling, or visualizing a peaceful environment in the mind. A safe space allows for the processing of emotions in a controlled and nurturing environment, where the individual can explore their feelings without the pressure of immediate reaction. This space can also serve as a retreat when triggers become overwhelming, providing an opportunity to reset and regain emotional balance.

Building Emotional Resilience through Regular Practice

Coping with emotional triggers is not about eliminating them but about building resilience so that they have less impact over time. Regular mindfulness practice, including meditation, mindful movement, and self-compassion exercises, strengthens emotional resilience by fostering a greater sense of inner stability and awareness. As individuals become more attuned to their emotional responses and more skilled in managing them, triggers become less daunting and easier to navigate. Over time, this resilience leads to a more balanced and grounded emotional state, where triggers are met with understanding and composure rather than reactivity.

The Importance of Patience and Compassion

Coping with emotional triggers is a gradual process that requires patience and self-compassion. It is important to acknowledge that setbacks may occur and that progress might be slow at times. Mindfulness teaches the value of being kind to oneself during this journey, recognizing that managing triggers is a skill that takes time to develop. By approaching this process with compassion, individuals can reduce self-criticism and foster a more supportive internal environment. This, in turn, enhances the ability to cope with triggers effectively and maintain emotional well-being.

7.3 Building Resilience through Mindful Emotional Practices

Understanding Emotional Resilience

Emotional resilience refers to the capacity to adapt to and recover from adversity, stress, or challenging situations. It involves maintaining a stable emotional state despite difficulties and bouncing back from setbacks with a sense of strength and stability. Building resilience is crucial for navigating life's inevitable ups and downs, and mindfulness offers powerful practices to enhance this resilience. Emotional resilience is not about eliminating stress or adversity but about developing the skills and mindset to handle these challenges effectively.

Mindfulness Practices for Enhancing Resilience

Mindfulness practices cultivate a deeper awareness and acceptance of the present moment, which can significantly enhance emotional resilience. By training the mind to focus on the here and now, mindfulness helps individuals maintain a balanced perspective during stressful times. Practices such as mindfulness meditation, body scans, and mindful breathing teach individuals to observe their thoughts and emotions without becoming overwhelmed by them. This observational stance allows for a clearer understanding of emotional responses and fosters a sense of calm and control. Regular mindfulness practice strengthens the ability to remain grounded and resilient in the face of adversity.

Developing a Growth Mindset through Mindfulness

A growth mindset, the belief that abilities and qualities can be developed through effort and learning, is a key component of emotional resilience. Mindfulness supports the development of a growth mindset by promoting self-awareness and self-compassion. When individuals practice mindfulness, they become more aware of their thought patterns and are better able to challenge negative self-beliefs or fixed mindsets. For example, mindfulness can help individuals recognize and reframe thoughts such as "I can't handle this" to "I am capable of learning and growing from this experience." This shift in mindset enhances resilience by fostering a positive and adaptive approach to challenges.

Using Mindful Reflection to Learn from Experiences

Mindful reflection involves taking time to thoughtfully consider and learn from past experiences. This practice helps individuals gain insights into their emotional responses and behaviors, which can inform future actions. Reflecting mindfully on challenging situations allows individuals to identify what strategies were effective and what could be improved. For example, after experiencing a stressful event, one might use mindful reflection to explore how they responded, what emotions were triggered, and how their mindfulness practices helped or could be adjusted. This reflective process promotes continuous personal growth and strengthens resilience by enhancing self-awareness and adaptive coping strategies.

Integrating Mindfulness into Daily Life for Consistent Resilience

To build long-term emotional resilience, it is important to integrate mindfulness into daily routines rather than relying on it as a reactive tool during crises. Incorporating mindfulness into everyday activities—such as eating, walking, or even working—helps to create a consistent foundation of awareness and presence. This integration fosters a steady sense of calm and stability, making it easier to handle stressful situations when they arise. Daily mindfulness practices, such as setting aside time for meditation or taking mindful breaks throughout the day, contribute to overall emotional resilience by reinforcing the skills of observation, acceptance, and self-regulation.

Cultivating Self-Compassion as a Resilience Builder

Self-compassion, the practice of treating oneself with kindness and understanding during difficult times, is a crucial aspect of emotional resilience. Mindfulness and self-compassion are closely linked, as mindfulness teaches individuals to observe their emotions and experiences with acceptance, while self-compassion provides a supportive and nurturing response. By practicing self-compassion, individuals can address their emotional struggles with gentleness and empathy, rather than harsh self-criticism. This compassionate approach enhances resilience by reducing the impact of negative emotions and fostering a sense of inner support and encouragement.

Building Social Support through Mindfulness

Emotional resilience is not only an individual endeavor but also involves building and maintaining supportive relationships. Mindfulness can enhance social support by fostering better communication and empathy with others. Practices such as mindful listening and empathetic engagement improve the quality of interactions and strengthen social connections. When individuals practice mindfulness, they become more attuned to their emotional states and those of others, which enhances their ability to offer and receive support. Strong social networks contribute to resilience by providing additional resources, perspectives, and encouragement during challenging times.

Long-Term Benefits of Mindful Emotional Practices

The long-term benefits of building resilience through mindful emotional practices are profound. Individuals who regularly engage in mindfulness and related practices often experience greater emotional stability, improved stress management, and a more positive outlook on life. This enhanced resilience not only helps individuals cope with immediate challenges but also fosters a greater sense of overall well-being and satisfaction. By continually practicing mindfulness, individuals develop the skills and mindset necessary to navigate life's difficulties with confidence and grace, leading to a more resilient and fulfilling life.

Chapter 8: Living a Fulfilling Life through Mindful Emotional Intelligence

Defining a Fulfilling Life

A fulfilling life is characterized by a deep sense of satisfaction, purpose, and well-being. It involves not only achieving personal goals but also cultivating meaningful relationships, experiencing personal growth, and engaging in activities that align with one's values and passions. Mindful emotional intelligence plays a crucial role in living a fulfilling life by enhancing self-awareness, emotional regulation, and interpersonal relationships. Through mindful practices, individuals can create a more harmonious and enriched life, where they are better equipped to navigate challenges, embrace opportunities, and connect deeply with themselves and others.

The Role of Self-Awareness in Fulfillment

Self-awareness is a cornerstone of mindful emotional intelligence and a key component of a fulfilling life. It involves a clear understanding of one's emotions, strengths, weaknesses, values, and goals. By cultivating self-awareness through mindfulness practices, individuals gain insights into their true selves, enabling them to make more informed and authentic decisions. This clarity allows for a greater alignment between one's actions and values, leading to a more meaningful and satisfying life. Self-awareness also fosters personal growth by highlighting areas for improvement and opportunities for development, further contributing to a sense of fulfillment.

Embracing Emotional Regulation for a Balanced Life

Emotional regulation, the ability to manage and healthily respond to emotions, is essential for maintaining balance and fulfillment. Mindfulness enhances emotional regulation by providing tools and techniques to navigate emotions with awareness and acceptance. This ability to regulate emotions allows individuals to handle stress, adversity, and interpersonal conflicts more effectively. By responding to emotions with mindfulness rather than reactivity, individuals can maintain a sense of equilibrium and resilience, which contributes to overall life satisfaction and well-being. Emotional regulation also supports healthier relationships and a more positive outlook on life.

Building and Maintaining Meaningful Relationships

Meaningful relationships are a significant aspect of a fulfilling life, and mindful emotional intelligence enhances the quality of these connections. Mindful communication, active listening, and empathy are crucial for fostering strong and supportive relationships. By practicing mindfulness in interactions with others, individuals become more present and attentive, leading to deeper and more authentic connections. Additionally, mindfulness helps individuals manage conflicts and navigate relationships with compassion and understanding, contributing to a more harmonious and fulfilling social life. Building and maintaining meaningful relationships through mindful practices enriches one's life and provides a sense of belonging and support.

Pursuing Personal Growth and Purpose

A fulfilling life often involves pursuing personal growth and a sense of purpose. Mindful emotional intelligence supports this pursuit by fostering a growth mindset and encouraging self-reflection. By being aware of one's passions, strengths, and goals, individuals can set meaningful objectives and work towards them with intention and resilience. Mindfulness practices such as goal setting, visualization, and reflective journaling help individuals stay focused on their aspirations and navigate challenges with clarity. Pursuing personal growth and purpose through mindful emotional intelligence leads to a more rewarding and purposeful life, where individuals can achieve their full potential and find deep satisfaction.

Balancing Achievement and Contentment

Achieving personal and professional goals is important for a fulfilling life, but it is equally crucial to cultivate contentment with the present moment. Mindful emotional intelligence helps individuals strike a balance between striving for success and appreciating what they have. By practicing mindfulness, individuals learn to enjoy the journey rather than solely focusing on outcomes. This balance between achievement and contentment promotes a sense of fulfillment and prevents burnout or dissatisfaction. Mindfulness also encourages gratitude and appreciation for the present moment, enhancing overall well-being and life satisfaction.

Integrating Mindfulness into Daily Life

Living a fulfilling life through mindful emotional intelligence involves integrating mindfulness into daily routines and activities. This integration ensures that mindfulness is not just a practice but a way of life. Mindful living includes being present in everyday moments, practicing gratitude, and approaching challenges with a mindful attitude. Incorporating mindfulness into daily activities, such as mindful eating, mindful walking, or mindful work practices, helps maintain a consistent sense of awareness and presence. This ongoing integration supports emotional well-being and contributes to a more balanced and fulfilling life.

The Long-Term Impact of Mindful Emotional Intelligence

The long-term impact of cultivating mindful emotional intelligence is profound. Over time, individuals who practice mindfulness and emotional intelligence develop greater resilience, deeper self-awareness, and more meaningful relationships. These benefits contribute to a lasting sense of fulfillment and well-being. Mindful emotional intelligence also fosters a more positive and compassionate outlook on life, enhancing overall life satisfaction. By continuously applying mindful practices and principles, individuals can create a fulfilling life characterized by inner peace, personal growth, and meaningful connections with others.

In summary, living a fulfilling life through mindful emotional intelligence involves embracing self-awareness, emotional regulation, and meaningful relationships. By integrating mindfulness into daily practices and pursuing personal growth with intention, individuals can achieve a deeper sense of satisfaction and well-being. Mindful emotional intelligence offers a powerful framework for navigating life's challenges and opportunities with grace and resilience. Embracing these practices leads to a more enriched and fulfilling life, where individuals can thrive emotionally, personally, and relationally.

8.1 Integrating Mindfulness and Emotional Intelligence into Daily Life

Creating a Mindful Routine

Integrating mindfulness and emotional intelligence into daily life begins with establishing a mindful routine. A mindful routine involves incorporating specific mindfulness practices into the regular rhythm of daily activities. This might include starting the day with a few minutes of meditation or mindful breathing to set a positive tone. Engaging in mindful eating, where one pays full attention to the flavors, textures, and sensations of food, can enhance the eating experience and promote better digestion. Integrating mindfulness into routine activities helps to anchor awareness in the present moment and fosters a sense of calm throughout the day. By making mindfulness a regular part of daily routines, individuals can create a foundation for emotional intelligence to flourish.

Mindful Work Practices

Applying mindfulness to work practices can significantly enhance productivity and emotional well-being. Mindful work practices involve approaching tasks with focused attention and presence, rather than multitasking or rushing through responsibilities. For instance, practicing single-tasking, where one focuses on completing one task at a time, can improve concentration and reduce stress. Mindful communication in the workplace, such as actively listening during meetings and responding thoughtfully to colleagues, fosters better interpersonal relationships and collaboration. Additionally, incorporating short mindful breaks throughout the workday, such as a brief walk or a few minutes of deep breathing, can help manage stress and maintain emotional balance. These mindful work practices contribute to a more effective and satisfying work environment.

Mindful Emotional Check-Ins

Regular emotional check-ins are an essential part of integrating emotional intelligence into daily life. An emotional check-in involves pausing to assess one's emotional state and identify any underlying feelings or concerns. This practice can be done at various times throughout the day, such as during breaks, before or after meetings, or at the end of the day. By taking a moment to reflect on emotions, individuals can gain insight into their emotional landscape and address any issues that may arise. This practice promotes self-awareness and allows for timely emotional regulation. Keeping a journal for these emotional check-ins can further enhance self-understanding and track emotional patterns over time.

Mindful Relationship Practices

Integrating mindfulness and emotional intelligence into relationships involves fostering awareness, empathy, and effective communication. Mindful relationship practices include being fully present during interactions with others, listening actively, and responding with empathy and compassion. Practicing mindful listening means giving undivided attention to the speaker, acknowledging their feelings, and providing thoughtful responses. Additionally, mindfulness can help manage conflicts by encouraging calm and reflective responses rather than reactive ones. Regularly expressing appreciation and gratitude in relationships also strengthens emotional connections and fosters a positive and supportive environment. By incorporating these practices, individuals can enhance the quality of their relationships and build stronger emotional bonds.

Setting Boundaries Mindfully

Setting boundaries is a crucial aspect of emotional intelligence and personal well-being. Mindful boundary-setting involves clearly defining and communicating personal limits respectfully and assertively. This practice helps to maintain a healthy balance between personal needs and external demands. For example, setting boundaries at work might involve establishing limits on work hours or taking breaks when needed. In personal relationships, it might involve communicating needs and expectations to ensure mutual respect and understanding. Mindfulness supports boundary-setting by promoting awareness of one's needs and the ability to express them calmly and clearly. Establishing and maintaining boundaries mindfully protects emotional well-being and prevents burnout or resentment.

Practicing Gratitude and Positive Reflection

Incorporating gratitude and positive reflection into daily life enhances emotional intelligence and overall well-being. Mindful gratitude involves regularly acknowledging and appreciating the positive aspects of life, whether big or small. This practice can be integrated into daily routines by keeping a gratitude journal, where one writes down things they are grateful for each day. Positive reflection involves reviewing and celebrating personal achievements, strengths, and progress. By focusing on the positive aspects of life and reflecting on accomplishments, individuals can cultivate a more optimistic and resilient mindset. This practice not only boosts emotional well-being but also reinforces a sense of fulfillment and satisfaction.

Using Mindfulness to Manage Daily Stress

Daily stressors are an inevitable part of life, and mindfulness provides valuable tools for managing them effectively. Techniques such as mindful breathing, progressive muscle relaxation, and mindful observation can help reduce stress and promote relaxation. For instance, practicing deep breathing exercises during stressful moments can activate the body's relaxation response and calm the mind. Additionally, mindfulness techniques for managing stress can be applied to specific situations, such as handling challenging conversations or managing deadlines. By using mindfulness to address stressors, individuals can maintain emotional balance and enhance their overall resilience.

Continual Practice and Reflection

Integrating mindfulness and emotional intelligence into daily life is an ongoing process that requires continual practice and reflection. Regularly revisiting and adjusting mindfulness practices based on personal experiences and needs helps to sustain progress and growth.

Setting aside time for regular mindfulness sessions, reflecting on emotional experiences, and seeking feedback from trusted sources can support ongoing development. Engaging in mindfulness-based workshops or reading materials on emotional intelligence can also provide additional insights and techniques. By making mindfulness and emotional intelligence a lifelong commitment, individuals can continually enhance their well-being and lead a more fulfilling life.

In summary, integrating mindfulness and emotional intelligence into daily life involves creating a mindful routine, applying mindful work practices, conducting regular emotional check-ins, and fostering mindful relationships. It also includes setting boundaries, practicing gratitude, managing daily stress, and committing to continual practice and reflection. By embracing these practices, individuals can cultivate a more balanced and fulfilling life, characterized by greater self-awareness, emotional resilience, and meaningful connections. Mindful integration enhances overall well-being and supports a life of purpose and satisfaction.

8.2 Creating a Balanced and Fulfilling Life

Defining Balance and Fulfillment

Creating a balanced and fulfilling life involves harmonizing various aspects of one's existence to achieve a sense of overall well-being and satisfaction. Balance refers to the equilibrium between different areas of life, such as work, relationships, personal growth, and leisure. Fulfillment, on the other hand, encompasses a deep sense of purpose, achievement, and contentment. Together, balance and fulfillment contribute to a life that feels rich, meaningful, and satisfying. Achieving this harmony requires intentional effort, self-awareness, and a commitment to aligning one's actions with core values and goals.

Setting Clear Goals and Priorities

To create a balanced and fulfilling life, it is essential to set clear goals and priorities. Goals provide direction and purpose, while priorities help to allocate time and energy effectively. Setting specific, measurable, achievable, relevant, and time-bound (SMART) goals ensures clarity and focus. Prioritizing these goals based on personal values and long-term vision helps to maintain balance across different life domains. For example, balancing career aspirations with personal relationships and self-care involves setting priorities that align with one's overall vision of a fulfilling life. Regularly reviewing and adjusting goals and priorities ensures that they remain relevant and aligned with evolving aspirations.

Managing Time Effectively

Effective time management is crucial for maintaining balance and achieving fulfillment. Creating a structured schedule that allocates time for work, personal activities, relationships, and self-care helps to prevent overwhelmed and burnout. Techniques such as time blocking, setting deadlines, and using productivity tools can enhance time management. Additionally, incorporating regular breaks and downtime into the schedule supports overall well-being and prevents fatigue. Mindful time management involves being present and focused during tasks, as well as making conscious choices about how to spend time. This approach promotes efficiency and ensures that time is dedicated to activities that contribute to a balanced and fulfilling life.

Nurturing Physical and Mental Health

Physical and mental health are foundational to creating a balanced and fulfilling life. Prioritizing self-care through regular exercise, healthy eating, and sufficient sleep supports overall well-being and energy levels. Additionally, mental health practices such as mindfulness, stress management, and seeking professional support when needed are essential for maintaining emotional balance. Integrating activities that promote relaxation and mental clarity, such as meditation, yoga, or hobbies, contributes to a sense of fulfillment. By addressing both physical and mental health needs, individuals can enhance their capacity to lead a balanced and satisfying life.

Cultivating Meaningful Relationships

Meaningful relationships are a key component of a fulfilling life. Nurturing connections with family, friends, and colleagues fosters a sense of belonging and support. Building and maintaining these relationships involves effective communication, active listening, and mutual respect. Investing time and effort in relationships strengthens emotional bonds and contributes to overall life satisfaction. Additionally, seeking and offering support within relationships enhances emotional resilience and fulfillment. Engaging in shared activities and creating positive experiences together further enriches relationships and contributes to a balanced and fulfilling life.

Pursuing Personal Growth and Learning

Personal growth and continuous learning are integral to a fulfilling life. Pursuing new interests, skills, and experiences contributes to a sense of achievement and self-improvement. Setting aside time for personal development, such as taking courses, reading, or engaging in creative pursuits, fosters a growth mindset and enhances overall satisfaction. Embracing challenges and stepping out of comfort zones promotes resilience and personal evolution. By prioritizing personal growth, individuals create opportunities for enrichment and fulfillment, contributing to a balanced and purposeful life.

Finding Joy and Appreciation in Everyday Moments

Finding joy and appreciation in everyday moments is essential for creating a fulfilling life. Practicing mindfulness and gratitude helps individuals to recognize and savor positive experiences and simple pleasures. Incorporating rituals or practices that bring joy, such as spending time in nature, engaging in hobbies, or connecting with loved ones, enhances daily well-being. Celebrating small victories and expressing gratitude for the positive aspects of life reinforces a sense of fulfillment and contentment. By focusing on the present moment and appreciating life's blessings, individuals can cultivate a more balanced and satisfying existence.

Balancing Work and Personal Life

Achieving a balance between work and personal life is crucial for overall fulfillment. Setting boundaries between work and personal time helps to prevent burnout and ensures that time is dedicated to both professional and personal interests. Strategies such as flexible work arrangements, setting clear work hours, and prioritizing personal time contribute to a healthier work-life balance. Engaging in leisure activities, spending quality time with family and friends, and pursuing hobbies outside of work fosters a well-rounded and fulfilling life. By maintaining this balance, individuals can experience greater satisfaction and well-being.

Reflecting and Adjusting Regularly

Creating a balanced and fulfilling life is an ongoing process that requires regular reflection and adjustment. Periodically evaluating one's goals, priorities, and well-being helps to identify areas for improvement and make necessary changes. Reflecting on personal experiences, achievements, and challenges provides valuable insights into what contributes to fulfillment. Adjusting goals and routines based on these reflections ensures that one's life remains aligned with evolving aspirations and needs. This ongoing process of reflection and adjustment supports a dynamic and fulfilling life, where individuals continuously grow and adapt.

In conclusion, creating a balanced and fulfilling life involves setting clear goals, managing time effectively, nurturing physical and mental health, cultivating meaningful relationships, pursuing personal growth, and finding joy in everyday moments. Balancing work and personal life and engaging in regular reflection and adjustment are also key components. By integrating these practices, individuals can achieve a harmonious and enriched existence, characterized by overall well-being, satisfaction, and purpose. Embracing a balanced and fulfilling life is a continuous journey that requires intention, self-awareness, and a commitment to personal growth and well-being.

8.3 The Long-Term Benefits of Mindful Emotional Intelligence

Enhanced Emotional Resilience

One of the most significant long-term benefits of mindful emotional intelligence is enhanced emotional resilience. Emotional resilience refers to the ability to adapt to stress, overcome adversity, and recover from challenges. Mindfulness practices, such as meditation and mindful breathing, strengthen this resilience by helping individuals manage their emotional responses and maintain a balanced perspective. Over time, individuals with mindful emotional intelligence become better equipped to handle life's ups and downs with grace and composure. This resilience not only improves their capacity to cope with difficult situations but also contributes to a more stable and fulfilling emotional life.

Improved Relationship Quality

Mindful emotional intelligence significantly enhances the quality of relationships over the long term. By fostering greater self-awareness, empathy, and effective communication, individuals are better able to connect with others on a deeper level. Mindful practices help individuals approach relationships with more patience, understanding, and compassion. This results in more meaningful and harmonious interactions with family, friends, and colleagues. Additionally, improved emotional intelligence contributes to healthier conflict resolution and stronger interpersonal bonds, leading to more satisfying and supportive relationships.

Increased Self-Awareness and Personal Growth

Long-term engagement with mindful emotional intelligence promotes increased self-awareness and personal growth. Through regular mindfulness practices, individuals gain a deeper understanding of their emotions, thoughts, and behaviors. This heightened self-awareness allows for more intentional and authentic living. As individuals become more attuned to their inner experiences, they are better positioned to identify areas for personal development and pursue growth opportunities. This ongoing process of self-discovery and improvement contributes to a more fulfilling and purposeful life.

Greater Life Satisfaction and Well-Being

Individuals who consistently practice mindful emotional intelligence experience greater life satisfaction and overall well-being. By cultivating emotional balance, managing stress effectively, and fostering positive relationships, individuals enhance their quality of life. Mindfulness practices encourage a focus on the present moment and appreciation for life's simple pleasures, which boosts overall contentment. This increased sense of satisfaction extends to various aspects of life, including work, personal achievements, and social interactions. As a result, individuals with mindful emotional intelligence often report higher levels of happiness and fulfillment.

Enhanced Decision-Making Skills

Mindful emotional intelligence contributes to improved decision-making skills over time. By increasing self-awareness and emotional regulation, individuals are better able to make informed and balanced decisions.

Mindfulness helps to reduce impulsivity and reactivity, allowing for more thoughtful consideration of options and consequences. This leads to more effective problem-solving and decision-making in both personal and professional contexts. As individuals become more adept at making decisions aligned with their values and goals, they experience greater success and satisfaction in their endeavors.

Reduced Stress and Better Health

The long-term practice of mindful emotional intelligence is associated with reduced stress and better health outcomes. Mindfulness techniques, such as relaxation exercises and mindful awareness, help lower stress levels and improve overall well-being. By managing stress effectively and promoting a positive mindset, individuals can experience lower levels of anxiety and depression. Additionally, the benefits of mindfulness extend to physical health, with research indicating that regular mindfulness practice can lower blood pressure, improve immune function, and support healthy lifestyle choices. This holistic approach to stress management contributes to better long-term health and vitality.

Stronger Emotional Regulation

Effective emotional regulation is a key benefit of mindful emotional intelligence. Over time, mindfulness practices help individuals develop greater control over their emotional responses. This enhanced regulation allows individuals to navigate complex emotions with greater ease and stability. By managing emotions more effectively, individuals are less likely to experience emotional overwhelm or react impulsively. This improved emotional control contributes to healthier relationships, better stress management, and overall emotional well-being.

Increased Empathy and Compassion

Mindful emotional intelligence fosters increased empathy and compassion, both towards oneself and others. Regular mindfulness practice enhances one's ability to understand and connect with the emotions of others, leading to more empathetic and supportive interactions. This increased empathy contributes to stronger interpersonal relationships and a greater sense of community. Additionally, self-compassion practices promote a more positive and forgiving attitude towards oneself, reducing self-criticism and enhancing overall emotional well-being.

Long-Term Personal Fulfillment

Ultimately, the long-term benefits of mindful emotional intelligence contribute to a deeper sense of personal fulfillment. By fostering emotional resilience, improving relationships, enhancing self-awareness, and promoting overall well-being, individuals create a more balanced and satisfying life. The ongoing practice of mindfulness and emotional intelligence supports continuous personal growth and a more meaningful existence. As individuals cultivate these skills, they experience a greater sense of purpose, achievement, and contentment, leading to a fulfilling and enriched life.

In conclusion, the long-term benefits of mindful emotional intelligence are profound and multifaceted. Enhanced emotional resilience, improved relationship quality, increased self-awareness, greater life satisfaction, and better health are just a few of the many advantages. By embracing and practicing mindful emotional intelligence, individuals can create a more balanced, fulfilling, and meaningful life. The ongoing commitment to mindfulness and emotional intelligence fosters personal growth, strengthens relationships, and enhances overall well-being, leading to a richer and more satisfying life experience.

Conclusion

In a world that often feels chaotic and fast-paced, the pursuit of a balanced and fulfilling life can seem like an elusive goal. However, through the practice of mindful emotional intelligence, we can find a path to harmony and satisfaction that aligns with our deepest values and aspirations. This book has explored how integrating mindfulness practices with emotional intelligence can transform our lives, offering tools and insights to navigate the complexities of our emotions with grace and resilience.

Mindful emotional intelligence begins with a foundational understanding of emotional intelligence itself—recognizing and managing our emotions while fostering empathy and effective communication. By coupling this with mindfulness, we deepen our capacity for self-awareness and emotional regulation. Mindfulness empowers us to observe our thoughts and feelings without judgment, allowing for a clearer perspective and more intentional responses.

As we delve into the techniques for cultivating self-awareness through mindfulness, we discover the profound impact of self-reflection and emotional understanding. Recognizing and embracing our emotions, rather than avoiding or suppressing them, enriches our experience and facilitates personal growth. This heightened self-awareness not only enhances our well-being but also transforms how we interact with others, leading to more compassionate and empathetic relationships.

Practicing emotional regulation with mindfulness equips us with strategies to manage stress, anxiety, and negative emotions effectively. Techniques such as mindful breathing and thoughtful response rather than reaction become invaluable tools for maintaining balance amidst life's challenges. These practices build resilience, enabling us to face difficulties with a composed and centered approach.

Compassion, both towards ourselves and others, is a cornerstone of mindful emotional intelligence. By nurturing self-compassion, we create a foundation for greater self-acceptance and emotional well-being. Loving-kindness meditation and empathy practices further enrich our relationships, fostering a supportive and understanding environment that enhances our sense of connection and fulfillment.

The development of social skills through mindful emotional intelligence brings about significant improvements in communication, empathy, and interpersonal dynamics. By integrating mindful communication and empathy into our interactions, we build stronger and more meaningful connections, enriching our personal and professional relationships.

Overcoming emotional challenges with mindfulness offers a pathway to greater resilience and adaptability. By addressing negative emotions and coping with triggers mindfully, we develop the tools to navigate adversity with greater ease and maintain emotional stability. Building resilience through mindful practices equips us to handle life's fluctuations with a balanced and constructive approach.

Ultimately, living a fulfilling life through mindful emotional intelligence involves embracing balance and intentionality in all aspects of our existence. By integrating mindfulness into daily routines, managing time effectively, nurturing relationships, and pursuing personal growth, we create a life of purpose and satisfaction. The long-term benefits of mindful emotional intelligence—enhanced resilience, improved relationships, greater self-awareness, and overall well-being—underscore its profound impact on our lives.

As you conclude this journey through mindful emotional intelligence, remember that this practice is not a destination but an ongoing process. The path to balance and fulfillment is one of continuous growth and reflection. By embracing the principles and practices outlined in this book, you embark on a lifelong journey of self-discovery, compassion, and enriched living. May you find joy and satisfaction in every moment, and may the wisdom of mindful emotional intelligence guide you toward a life of profound fulfillment and harmony.